Taiwan's 2001 Legislative, Magistrates and Mayors Election

Further Consolidating Democracy?

East Asian Institute (EAI)
Contemporary China Series No. 33

Taiwan's 2001 Legislative, Magistrates and Mayors Election

Further Consolidating Democracy?

John F Copper

Rhodes College, USA

World Scientific
New Jersey • London • Singapore • Hong Kong

SINGAPORE UNIVERSITY PRESS
NATIONAL UNIVERSITY OF SINGAPORE

Published by

World Scientific Publishing Co. Pte. Ltd.
5 Toh Tuck Link, Singapore 596224
USA office: Suite 202, 1060 Main Street, River Edge, NJ 07661
UK office: 57 Shelton Street, Covent Garden, London WC2H 9HE

and

Singapore University Press Pte. Ltd.
Yusof Ishak House, National University of Singapore
10 Kent Ridge Crescent, Singapore 119260

TAIWAN'S 2001 LEGISLATIVE, MAGISTRATES AND MAYORS ELECTION:
Further Consolidating Democracy
EAI Occasional Paper No. 33
Copyright © 2002 by World Scientific Publishing Co. Pte. Ltd. and
Singapore University Press Pte. Ltd.

All rights reserved. This book, or parts thereof, may not be reproduced in any form or by any means, electronic or mechanical, including photocopying, recording or any information storage and retrieval system now known or to be invented, without written permission from the Publishers.

For photocopying of material in this volume, please pay a copying fee through the Copyright Clearance Center, Inc., 222 Rosewood Drive, Danvers, MA 01923, USA. In this case permission to photocopy is not required from the publishers.

ISBN 981-238-193-7

Printed in Singapore.

CONTENTS

Taiwan's 2001 Legislative, Magistrates and Mayors Election: Further Consolidating Democracy?
John F. Copper

Introduction	1
Pre-Election Politics	6
Political Party Line-up and Platforms	24
The Campaign	39
The Election Results	53
Conclusions	67

TAIWAN'S 2001 LEGISLATIVE, MAGISTRATES AND MAYORS ELECTION: FURTHER CONSOLIDATING DEMOCRACY?

John F. Copper

Introduction

On December 1, 2001, voters in Taiwan (officially known as the Republic of China) cast ballots to elect a new Legislative Yuan, or the country's lawmaking body of government, plus mayors (though not for Taipei and Kaohsiung, which are defined as metropolitan cites and have separate elections) and county magistrates island-wide. The part of the election to decide Taiwan's new legislature constituted Taiwan's eleventh competitive national election (its twelfth if the 1994 election of Taiwan's provincial governor, provincial assembly, metropolitan mayors and city councils is counted, which by most measures was a national election).[1] It was Taiwan's eighth competitive legislative election beginning with the contest in 1980.

---

[1] For an assessment of Taiwan's previous important elections, see John F. Copper with George P. Chen, *Taiwan's Elections: Political Development and Democratization in the Republic of China* (Baltimore: University of Maryland School of Law, 1984); John F. Copper, *Taiwan's Recent Elections: Fulfilling the Democratic Promise* (Baltimore:

More important, this election was the first expression of the electorate's view of politics, political candidates, and political parties in Taiwan following the watershed presidential election of March 2000. That election resulted in the ruling Nationalist Party or Kuomintang (KMT) losing control of the executive branch of government for the first time ever, while forcing it to yield the presidency to the candidate of the Democratic Progressive Party (DPP).[2] Taiwan's new chief executive, Chen Shui-bian, and his party as well, were on trial from virtually day one. His administration was plagued by divided government, which made it extremely difficult to rule. This and other difficulties affected the nation's economy and its foreign relations. Leading up to this election the electorate would, it was thought, decide who was to blame for this state of affairs and help correct it.

Before the election, the outcome of the voting was also seen as possibly deciding the future of one or more, perhaps all, of Taiwan's political parties. The New Party, formed in 1993 from the KMT's "non-mainstream faction" (opponents of President Lee Teng-hui and supporters of one China), had been in eclipse for a number of years. Some predicted this election would mark its demise. James Soong, who ran for president as an independent in 2000 and came in second in the voting, formed a new party, the People First Party (PFP),

---

University of Maryland School of Law, 1990); John F. Copper, *Taiwan's 1991 and 1992 Non-Supplemental Elections: Reaching a Higher State of Democracy* (Lanham, MD: University Press of America, 1994); John F. Copper, *Taiwan's Mid-1990s Elections: Taking the Final Steps to Democracy* (Westport, CT: Praeger Publisher, 1998); John F. Copper, *Taiwan's 1998 Legislative Yuan, Metropolitan Mayoral and City Council Elections: Confirming and Consolidating Democracy in the Republic of China* (Baltimore: University of Maryland School of Law, 1999) and John F. Copper, *Taiwan's 2000 Presidential and Vice Presidential Elections: Consolidating Democracy and Creating a New Era of Politics* (Baltimore: University of Maryland School of Law, 2000).

[2] See Copper, *Taiwan's 2000 Presidential and Vice Presidential Elections* for details.

immediately after the election. His party was on trial in this election. If it did well, the conventional wisdom went, it would become an established part of the political landscape and could develop a good organization, sources of funding, etc. Another new party was founded during the run-up to the election by Huang Chu-wen, a surrogate of former president Lee Teng-hui, and supporters of Lee, named the Taiwan Solidarity Union (TSU). Lee and the TSU condemned political gridlock, which they charged the KMT and PFP had caused, and sought to succor President Chen and the DPP. Lee and the TSU aimed to recruit members of the Nationalist Party that had remained loyal to Lee, including some members of the legislature, and appealed to pro-localization (those favoring Taiwan's separation from China) KMT voters. The KMT, which pundits were sure would lose its majority in the Legislative Yuan, was apprehensive of its future. It was a party in turmoil. Both the PFP and the TSU were encroaching on its membership. The KMT's situation was so grave, in fact, that some of its leaders suggested this election might tell whether or not the party was in serious or permanent decline.[3]

At stake also were the political futures of the often-discussed top presidential candidates — though none of them was currently running for any office.[4] President Chen Shui-bian would certainly run for another presidential term. If his party did well in this election his chances would be much improved. James Soong and Lien Chan were seen as likely candidates for president in 2004. Taipei Mayor Ma Ying-jeou was seen as a possible candidate, though how the election might affect his political career was not at all lucid; a poor showing by the KMT, some said, might result in party members calling on

---

[3] There were frequently heard suggestions of that after the 2000 election. It was again discussed when the party reregistered its membership later.

[4] There was an exception in that James Soong's name was listed as an at-large candidate for the PFP. He was not elected and most observers felt that he did not want to be. More details on this are cited below.

him to take the job of party chairman, though this was generally seen as speculation.[5]

The election would also say something about the nation's perception of the 78-year old former President Lee Teng-hui and his future political role in Taiwan, if indeed he was to have one. Many of Taiwan's citizens had great respect for Lee based on accomplishments during his twelve-year presidency. He was known fondly as "Mr. Democracy." Many also applauded his efforts to establish the TSU. Lee would surely increase his political influence and play a greater role as ex-president if the TSU did well, especially if it could help the DPP win a majority in the Legislative Yuan or could build one with the help of a few independents or KMT defectors after the election. Others opined that Lee should keep out of politics and that his strident and at times rude personal comments about Lien and Soong reflected the fact that he was senile. Clearly if the TSU did not do well Lee's political future would dim.

The future of a coalition government as well as its composition likewise appeared to hinge on the election results. President Chen promised coalition rule after the election. This indeed seemed necessary if he were to govern effectively and, more importantly, solve many of the nation's serious problems. On the other hand, "blocs" formed during the campaign that precluded or perhaps made it unnecessary for Chen to form a coalition. The DPP and the TSU were labeled the "green team" (the DPP's party color is green) and the KMT, PFP and the NP the "blue team" (for the KMT's color). If Chen's bloc or the green team won, then the coalition would already be built. If not, Chen would be compelled, it was said, to seek an agreement with either the PFP or the KMT and form a coalition comprised of ideologically opposing forces. How well this

---

[5] For details on Ma's hopes, see "Chung-hueh Lee, "Ma Ying-jeou: His prospects for future presidency look good," *Taiwan News*, August 4, 2001, p. 18.

might work was in doubt. Pundits said he might expect a backlash from his own party if he did this. It would also bring into question the role and even the future of the TSU. If the KMT and the PFP (the blue team) preformed well, Chen may, it was thought, have to relinquish many of the powers of the presidency. Another alternative was for Chen to build a non-party or extra-party grouping to avoid the problems of a coalition. He proposed that.

The matter of constructing a majority would, observers suggested, determine as well how Taiwan's Constitution would be amended and the political system changed. Being a mixed presidential-cabinet-parliamentary system and patently in need of repair, which direction it might take was at stake. A major DPP victory, even one in tandem with a good TSU performance, suggested a presidential system was more likely in Taiwan's future. Counterpointwise, if Chen's party performed poorly at the polls and he had to form a coalition with the opposition, he would have to surrender some presidential powers, perhaps pushing the system toward a parliamentary one. No coalition would likely result in continued or further gridlock.

Before the balloting the election was thought to turn on certain key issues. To many voters the election was a referendum on Taiwan's national identity and Taipei's relations with Beijing. After his 2000 election victory, President Chen tried to build a better relationship with Beijing and still maintain his Taiwan independence platform. This proved difficult. Chinese leaders regularly rebuffed Chen. Later, especially as this election approached, Chen sought to turn this into an advantage. Meanwhile decline in Taiwan's economy and the attraction of China (booming economically) were especially troubling for Chen and the DPP. "Black gold" (criminal involvement and corruption in politics), which had also been a campaign issue in 2000, and the management of the economy, which wasn't, were major election issues — with the various political parties putting very different spins on them. The national identity issue and black gold seemed to favor the DPP and the TSU. Taiwan's poor economic performance and its accompanying social problems seemed to benefit the opposition (meaning the KMT, PFP and the NP).[6]

Politics and many policy and legislative decisions had been put on hold for months before the election, with both sides thinking that the election would give them a mandate or at least some direction regarding policy positions to take later. Actions to deal with a bad economy and other matters were held in abeyance, which hurt the country and increased voter cynicism. The election campaign thus created an aura of a struggle for power, more than was usual during Taiwan's elections.[7]

The DPP won the election. So did the PFP. The KMT lost. The NP lost. The TSU's performance was difficult to assess. It did quite well for a new party; yet it did not get the number of seats that President Lee and other party members predicted. The green team did well, but did not get a majority. The blue team won a majority; but it was uncertain if it could keep it since some KMT legislators were thought likely to change parties. The possibility of an "alliance" (as Chen called his proposal to build a majority force transcending political parties) remained just that after the voting.

Pre-Election Politics

The starting point for assessing the 2001 campaign can best be delineated as the 2000 presidential election. In that contest, the opposition Democratic Progressive Party won a watershed and truly unexpected victory. The reasons for the victory are instructive in

---

[6] This was the commonly held view going into the election. These issues defined the green and blue teams.

[7] See John F. Copper, "Taiwan in Gridlock: Thoughts on the Chen Shui-bian Administration's First Eighteen Months," in John F. Copper (ed.), *Taiwan in Troubled Times: Essays on the Chen Shui-bian Presidency* (Singapore: World Scientific, 2002).

terms of the problems encountered by the political parties, their strategies, and the outcome of this election.

Prior to the 2000 election campaign Nationalist Party leaders and members disagreed over their presidential nominee, causing the party to divide disastrously as it turned out.[8] James Soong was the leading candidate as determined by various public opinion polls. Soong was born in China but grew up in Taiwan. After university he went to the United States. There he obtained a Ph.D. degree from Georgetown University, after which he returned to Taiwan. He immediately found a position in government where he rose quickly in rank and in 1979 became head of the Government Information Office. This high visibility job gave Soong notoriety, with many people commenting on his good looks and his ability to think and speak well. He went from there to the Department of Cultural Affairs of the party and in 1981 took the job of secretary general of the KMT. When President Chiang Ching-kuo died in early 1988, Soong put his career on the line, supporting Lee Teng-hui for the party chairmanship amidst efforts by the old guard to marginalize Lee.[9] In 1994, Soong was elected the first governor of Taiwan in an island-wide popularity contest that pitted Soong, a Mainland Chinese, against Taiwanese candidates. Soong won Taiwanese support based on his reputation for working together with local politicians, mostly Taiwanese, as Taiwan's appointed governor. His charisma, reputation for hard work and honesty, and, very important, President Lee Teng-hui campaigning for him, also gave him invaluable help.[10]

---

[8] See Copper, *Taiwan's 2000 President and Vice Presidential Election*, pp. 19–20.

[9] See John F. Copper, *Historical Dictionary of Taiwan (Republic of China) (Second Edition)* (Lanham, MD: Scarecrow Press, 2000), p. 67 for further details on Soong's career.

[10] See John F. Copper, *Taiwan's Mid-1990s Elections: Taking the Final Steps to Democracy* (Westport, CT: Praeger Publishers, 1998), chapter 2.

Subsequently Lee and Soong, whom Lee had referred to as "like a son," parted ways. More accurately they became bitter enemies. The reason or reasons for this are not known for sure. Some say that Lee became jealous of Soong. Others say Lee did not want a Mainland Chinese to succeed him. Clearly Soong had that ambition. It may have happened over other things.[11] Lee may have simply favored someone else. In any event, Lee supported his vice president, Lien Chan, to be the KMT's nominee.

Lien, like Soong, was born in China. But unlike Soong his parents were from Taiwan. Lien also studied in the United States (obtaining his Ph.D. in political science at the University of Chicago) and returned to Taiwan to become known as one of the country's best and brightest. In 1981 Lien was appointed minister of transportation and communications — the youngest minister ever. He later became minister of foreign affairs, governor of Taiwan Province, premier, and vice president. Meanwhile he was voted one of the party's vice chairmen. Clearly Lien was the most experienced person for the job. Lien was also good-looking, had a radio voice, and more important perhaps than all of this was Taiwanese.[12] Lien, however, did not have Soong's charisma or appeal to the common man and did not rank high in public popularity polls.

When the nomination was given to Lien at Lee's behest, Soong opted to run as an independent. This split the KMT. It also divided the conservative vote. During the campaign many KMT stalwarts thought that they could get Soong to drop out of the campaign. This, however, was unreasonable given the fact that Soong led in the polls over both the DPP's Chen Shui-bian and Lien by a huge margin, sometimes double. There was also hope that Soong could be brought

---

[11] Some said it involved a dispute over the Senkaku or Diaoyutai Islands north of Taiwan claimed by both Japan and China and Lee sided with Japan and Soong with China.

[12] See Copper, *Historical Dictionary of Taiwan*, pp. 118–19.

back into the party, but that was not realistic given the bitterness on both sides. The KMT (whether Lee did this or someone else, maybe Lien, is uncertain) released information about Soong's financial dealings when he was secretary general of the party that suggested embezzlement or stealing.[13] Soong's campaign was derailed as a result. Soong's opinion ratings fell badly. This boosted Chen's campaign and put him close to Soong or in the lead in the opinion polls during the late days of the campaign.[14]

Chen Shui-bian was educated locally and joined the opposition early in his career. Although from southern Taiwan, he served on the Taipei City Council and went from there to the legislature. In 1994, he won the Taipei mayoral election to become chief executive of the country's capital city. In 1998, he was defeated for a second term even though his record was a good one. This left him time to prepare to run for the 2000 presidential election.[15]

During the campaign, Chen, who had strongly backed Taiwan's independence throughout his political career, moderated his position on relations with China as well as on other issues. Late in the campaign he got Lee Yuan-tseh, a Nobel Prize winner and head of Taiwan's prestigious Academia Sinica, to endorse him, along with some noted business leaders. It was also widely rumored that President Lee Teng-hui was secretly supporting Chen, either because he had decided that Lien could not win or because he supported Taiwan independence (which Chen had long had a reputation for advocating). In any case, Chen's campaign peaked at the right time. Meanwhile, Soong and Lien both pursued a strategy of getting voters

---

[13] It was assumed by most observers during the presidential campaign that Lee was behind the release of party documents about Soong's alleged misuse of funds. Lee later denied this.

[14] Since publishing public opinion polls during the last days of a political campaign is prohibited in Taiwan it is uncertain whether Chen or Soong was ahead a week before the voting.

[15] See Copper, *Historical Dictionary of Taiwan*, pp. 53–54.

to dump the other in their favor so they could defeat Chen. Neither succeeded at this to the degree necessary to win and Chen Shui-bian got the presidency by default.[16]

After the election many KMT members and certainly more than before believed the reports of Lee wanting Chen to win. They were also bitter over the defeat. Right after the voting they gathered and demonstrated outside party headquarters demanding that Lee step down as chairman of the party (his term of office not coinciding with the presidency). The demonstrators soon turned to violence and became for all intents and purposes an angry mob. In this milieu Lee resigned. Lien inherited the job, but he was seen by many party people and even supporters as a "loser." After all he came out a distant third in the presidential race with the powerful KMT behind him. Others argued that leading the party and running for president were not the same, that Lien had the ability to run the party, and that there was no one else; therefore, Lien should stay — which he did.[17]

After the election pundits and leaders of all of the parties debated Chen's victory. Had there been provision for a run-off election in Taiwan's Constitution (as in many nations that have multiparty systems) Chen would not have been elected president. Soong would have certainly been the victor in a run-off contest.[18] But what did

---

[16] Copper, *Taiwan's 2000 Presidential and Vice-Presidential Election*, pp. 53–56.

[17] Other possible candidates for leadership of the KMT were excluded or lacked support in the party because they were Mainland Chinese, had only local support or did not have Lien's stature and experience.

[18] This was presumed in view of the fact that Soong received less than 3 percent of the popular vote than Chen and Lien was far behind. In a run-off election, especially with President Lee out of the picture at least temporarily, Soong would have gotten KMT votes. It is a noteworthy point that some KMT officials had intimated (it being illegal to publish opinion polls during the last ten days of the campaign) that Lien was leading Soong and that Soong voters should cast their ballots for Lien. Realizing after the election that this was not true, a sizeable number of voters were angry that they had not voted for Soong.

this mean? According to opinion polls taken just after the election the populace felt Chen should be the president.[19] Thus Chen had a mandate — but it was a weak questionable one.

A few days later, James Soong announced the formation of a new political party, the People First Party (PFP).[20] Soong's supporters, many of whom were still members of the KMT or those who had recently dropped their membership to help Soong, joined. This included a number of members of the Legislative Yuan. Hence Soong's new party was a force to reckon with even though it lacked money, grass roots organization, etc. This made Taiwan's political party system a three-party one, which gave the nation's party structure an element of inherent instability.[21]

Not only was Taiwan's three-party make-up the recipe for problems, the KMT was a party that had never been out of power and was certainly not ready to be an opposition party. Both its leaders as well as party members did not accept that role. Likewise the Democratic Progressive Party had never ruled and was not really schooled to do that. Many of its members were talented in opposition politics, some only in street politics. The DPP also suffered from factional difficulties that split the party on such salient issues as Taiwan independence versus closer relations with China.[22]

Another problem was the very nature of Taiwan's political system. It was a mixed presidential-cabinet-parliamentary system. The framers

---

[19] According to a United Daily News Press Group survey, 62.8 percent said they were satisfied with the election results. See Chiao-yen Lin and Will Clem, "Lien accepts responsibility for defeat," *Taiwan News*, March 19, 2000, p. 3.

[20] For information about the People First Party, see www.pfp.org

[21] For further details, see John F. Copper, "Taiwan in Gridlock," in Copper (ed.), *Taiwan in Troubled Times*, pp. 43–44.

[22] See Shelley Rigger, *From Opposition to Power: Taiwan's Democratic Progressive Party* (Boulder, Co: Lynne Rienner Publishers, 2001), chapter 5 and Chao Chien-min, "The Democratic Progressive Party's Factional Problems," in Copper (ed.), *Taiwan in Troubled Times*, pp. 101–122.

of the Constitution made the president weak, fearing authoritarian tendencies.[23] Chiang Kai-shek got around this by passing amendments to the Constitution called the "Temporary Provisions" and subsequently declaring martial law. However, his main means for ruling as a strong president was his hold on the ruling party. Thus, though martial law was later terminated and the Temporary Provisions cancelled, Chiang Ching-kuo and Lee Teng-hui were strong presidents because of heading the ruling Nationalist Party and controlling the legislature through the party.[24] Chen Shui-bian did not have this advantage and the system as a consequence reverted to one of a weak presidency.

Meanwhile, the response of the DPP and Chen's supporters to the victory was one of tremendous glee, optimism and high expectations. They had longed to put what they called "real democracy" into practice. They had high ideals. They were proud of soon-to-be president Chen Shui-bian. They looked forward to a new and better Taiwan. Many thought the DPP's agenda would soon be realized.

When Chen Shui-bian assumed the office in May, he and many others, most noticeably his most loyal supporters, got a bitter dose of realism. The DPP had only one-third of the seats in the legislature. Chen could not, hence, govern effectively without building a coalition and getting the support of one or both of the other parties. He thus promptly announced that he would not be a party president and resigned from official positions he held in the party. He appointed members of the opposition parties to his cabinet — most of them in fact.[25] His premier was a member of the KMT. Chen's approach to the situation was what most experts called rule by cohabitation after

---

[23] See Suisheng Zhao, *Power By Design: Constitution-Making in Nationalist China* (Honolulu: University of Hawaii Press, 1996).

[24] See Yu-shan Wu, "The ROC's Semi-Presidentialism at Work: Unstable Compromise, Not Cohabitation," *Issues and Studies*, September–October 2000, pp. 1–40.

[25] DPP members were 18 percent, KMT 33 percent and independents 50 percent.

the French system. He did not try to build a party coalition. He could not rely on either of the opposing parties; they were the enemy in the minds of most of his followers. In establishing a "cohabitation cabinet," moreover, Chen neglected to enlist the permission or approval of the parties from whence his appointments came. Rather than cooperate because of the appointments the other parties denounced their members for joining the government.[26]

In the meantime Chen tried to rule, outwardly and in style at least, as previous presidents had. This did not work well. Chen seemed to assume the system to be a presidential one, when it wasn't. The opposition acted as if they were in control and the system was a parliamentary one, which it wasn't either. Constitutionally speaking, Chen's political authority was more clearly delineated in the areas of foreign and security policy, neither of which was his forte. Chen had not studied abroad as many of Taiwan's leaders had. He did not speak English. Likewise for many of his supporters. Chen thus had to keep many KMT people in foreign affairs jobs.

Chen and the DPP had also long been at odds with the military. They had advocated cutting the defense budget and trammeling the authority of the military. The military and the intelligence communities were both staffed largely by Mainland Chinese at the top. Chen's support and voters were Taiwanese. Related to these problems, Chen's election angered China. Beijing continued to augment its military forces, especially those near the Taiwan Strait, and made frequent threats against Taiwan. In that context, Chen needed to increase defense spending and bolster morale in the military.[27]

---

[26] For details on the first few months of the Chen presidency, see Shelly Rigger, *From Opposition to Power: Taiwan's Democratic Progressive Party* (Boulder, CO: Lynne Rienner Publishers, 2001), chapter 9.

[27] See Maureen Pao, "A President under Siege," *Far Eastern Economic Review*, May 29, 2001, pp. 22–23. Also see Li Thian-hok, "Prepare the people for the coming invasion," *Taipei Times*, December 19, 2000 (online at www.taipeitimes.com)

The opposition's de facto weakness was in domestic affairs because Chen had a mandate to change many domestic policies. After all he won the election. Yet constitutionally that was not the case. Moreover the KMT, with help from the PFP and the NP when needed, controlled the Legislative Yuan. The result was a standoff and political gridlock.

Making the situation worse, both Chen and the opposition eyed the next elections, the legislative election in December 2001 and the next presidential election in 2004. Both frequently behaved as if they were campaigning. Chen sought to use the perks and advantages of his office to help his party. He continued to rail against "black gold" (corruption, vote buying and criminal involvement in politics) that was an election issue in 2000. Many said he did this in order to hurt the KMT and get even for the KMT's blocking his initiatives in the legislature. The opposition responded by passing legislation to embarrass Chen, divide his party and weaken his support bases. This included bills that threatened to bust the budget and give more to labor and other groups than Chen wanted in order to cast doubts about his presidency among his supporters and win over potential voters.[28]

Internecine political fighting of other sorts also began immediately after Chen assumed the presidency and escalated almost daily from that point. One of the most divisive and certainly one of the front and center issues was Taiwan's fourth nuclear power plant. Chen and the DPP for years had campaigned against nuclear energy. They promised to get rid of it if and when they were in power — which they never thought would be soon so their proposals were couched in radical language. Provisions for building the fourth plant, however, were passed into law by the previous government, contracts were signed,

---

[28] See "DPP should seek coalition partners," Taipei Times, December 29, 2000 (online at www.taipeitimes. com)

and building was underway. For all of these reasons, in the minds of the opposition, it could not be cancelled. But that is just what Chen did. And he did it without warning or negotiating with the opposition. The opposition's riposte was to impeach Chen.[29]

Constitutionally, however, impeachment is a difficult thing to do.[30] The opposition went ahead, but stopped short of following through. They managed to embarrass Chen, but they also hurt themselves. The imbroglio engendered cynicism among the populace and polarized Taiwan politically beyond what it was at the time. Chen had to appoint a new premier (the first one, Tang Fei, having favored the plant) and new cabinet members. Most were from the DPP, including the premier. Now even the pretense of cohabitation evaporated.[31]

Meanwhile, Chen thought he was obliged to fulfill another campaign promise or that this would help his presidency. During the campaign, candidate Chen dramatically altered his position on Taiwan independence and relations with China. Chen had been a vociferous supporter of Taiwan's independence throughout his political career. He argued for Taiwan's legal separation from China while a member of the Legislative Yuan. He had put a provision in the party's charter advocating Taiwan's independence. He was called a radical on the issue. But when campaigning for the presidency he abandoned his

---

[29] See Myra Lu, "Opposition reacts strongly to plant decision," *Taipei Journal*, November 3, 2000, p. 1. Chen met with Lien Chan shortly before he made the decision and did not warn Lien. Lien was angry and felt that Chen had deliberately caused him to lose face.

[30] According to the Constitution as amended, a vote of half of the legislature is required to propose impeachment, after which two-thirds is required to pass the motion. Then the bill goes to the National Assembly. The National Assembly, however, is not a functioning body and would have to be constituted in such a situation.

[31] See Wu, "The ROC's Semi-Presidentialism at Work," p. 10. For a delayed impact, see Maureen Pao, "A President under Siege," *Far Eastern Economic Review*, May 29, 2001, pp. 22–23.

past views, at least nominally, and called for better cross-strait relations. More specifically he proposed ending restraints on trade and other commercial relations with China and professed to seek negotiated settlements to other matters that had caused friction between the two sides.[32] Chen successfully defused the charges that he was a dangerous candidate (as the KMT had in previous elections generally portrayed the DPP).

In early 2000, the situation looked something like this: Middle-of-the-road voters accepted Chen's new moderate views on cross-strait relations at least inasmuch as they did not see a Chen presidency as dangerous. Chen's hard-line supporters ignored his change of colors, viewing him as the most pro-independence candidate while believing that his moderate views were simply expedient.

During the last days of the campaign, Beijing issued a "White Paper" on Taiwan. It read that China would employ military force against Taiwan if Taipei failed to negotiate reunification over an extended period of time. Heretofore Chinese leaders had threatened to attack Taiwan only if Taipei did something, i.e. allow foreign military bases on Taiwan, develop nuclear weapons, experience domestic turmoil, etc. This time one of the conditions was *not* doing something.[33] This alarmed people in Taiwan and angered voters. Ratcheting up the tension, just before the voting, China's Premier Zhu Rongji appeared on television and sternly warned Taiwan voters not to vote for the "candidate of independence" — meaning Chen Shui-bian.[34] Zhu's words sounded ominous. Voters were incensed.

---

[32] Chen, for example, proposed to end President Lee Teng-hui's policy of "go slow, be patient" regarding commercial relations with China.

[33] See "China's White Paper on Taiwan: The One-China Principle and the Taiwan Issue," Government Information Office (Taipei), February 21, 2000.

[34] All of Taiwan's newspapers carried Zhu's comments. The comments in full were cited in *Renmin Ribao* (People's Daily), March 16, 2000.

The result was a backlash and more voters cast their votes for Chen, not fewer.[35]

After the election, however, Chen sought better relations with Beijing. He continued to eschew Taiwan independence talk. He spoke instead of improving cross-strait ties. Chen appeared willing to compromise. As president-elect, Chen announced that he would establish "three links" (mail, trade and transportation) with China (as Beijing had proposed for some time) and get rid of Lee Teng-hui's "no haste, be patient" policy regarding cross-strait commercial relations. In addition, he pledged "four noes": no declaration of independence, no change in the country's name, no constitutional amendment to legalize Lee Teng-hui's "two state" theory (that Lee announced in July 1999 that incensed Chinese leaders) and no referendum on the issue of independence. He then added a fifth: He would not nullify the National Unification Guidelines.[36]

But, as viewed from China, Chen had not given up his basic position that Taiwan is not and should not be part of China. Chen brought to the presidency Taiwanese nationalism and in many ways signaled his supporters and others in Taiwan that he was still in favor of Taiwan's de jure independence. He invited Peng Ming-min (the "father of Taiwan independence") to officiate at his inauguration. During his address Chen used the term "Taiwan" thirty-five times and "Formosa" (an even stronger term conveying independence sentiment) twice; he used "Republic of China" but nine times. Former president Lee's mark on his administration was apparent. Many of Chen's appointments were recommended by Lee and most were known advocates of independence.[37]

---

[35] Copper, *Taiwan's 2000 Presidential and Vice Presidential Elections*, p. 40.

[36] For details, see Julian Baum, Dan Biers and Susan V. Lawrence, "Chen's Chance," *Far Eastern Economic Review*, March 30, 2001, pp. 18–19.

[37] See Cheong Ching, *Will Taiwan Break Away? The Rise of Taiwanese Nationalism* (Singapore: World Scientific, 2001), p. 26.

In response Beijing demanded proof of Chen's change of heart. Chinese leaders said that he had to agree to China's "one country, two systems" formula for Taiwan's reunification with China (used in bringing Hong Kong and Macao back into the fold) and the principle of one-China. They stuck to this adamantly. They made it a non-negotiable principle. Given the emotional nature of the "Taiwan issue" in China, especially among military leaders, and the fact that the United States and most other countries throughout the world supported the concept of one China, this was quite natural.[38]

China adopted a general policy of not dealing with Chen or members of his party until he agreed to Beijing's position. Since he would not, China regarded him as an enemy and would not negotiate with him or anyone from the DPP. Beijing's leaders ordered military maneuvers to send a message to Taipei. China also took punitive actions against Taiwan businesses operating in China that had supported Chen for the presidency or were known to advocate Taiwan's independence.[39]

President Chen thus could not fulfill his campaign promise of improving cross-strait relations. But expectations were low and Chen could boast of there being no crisis and poor relations being the product of Beijing's leaders' disagreements over Taiwan policy, the influence of the military, and China's lack of democracy. Thus strained or poor ties (except economic and there relations were good) did not constitute a major problem for the Chen Administration at least in the short term.

Chen was also compelled to do something about black gold as he had promised during the campaign. And he did. In some ways his performance was impressive. Within a few months of Chen becoming president, the Ministry of Justice had investigated 3,917 cases of

---

[38] See Sheng Lijun, "Taiwan at a Crossroads," *Asian Perspective*, Volume 25, No. 1 2001, p. 198.
[39] See Julian Baum, "Reality Check," *Far Eastern Economic Review*, July 6, 2000, p. 4.

corruption and 508 of these (involving 164 public officials) made it to court.[40] Chen's minister of justice soon garnered the highest public approval rating of any member of his cabinet. And the U.S. Department of State's annual human rights report read that in Taiwan "political and personal pressures on the judiciary decreased significantly."[41]

Some in the Chen Administration, however, began to question how good a political issue (read future campaign issue) black gold was and whether doggedly pursuing crime and corruption was wise in the context of tension with the opposition. Some DPP officials feared it would hurt them since the DPP was now the ruling party and had to deal with large amounts of public funds and would thus be vulnerable to the same criticisms it leveled against the KMT for many years regarding corruption.[42]

It was also true that public concern seemed to be slipping. After all, the KMT had been seen as a rich party that "bought" elections. Yet it lost the 2000 election badly. After Lee Teng-hui's removal from the chairmanship of the party, Liu Tai-ying, the well-known manager of KMT money, fell from the radar scope. Some also began to ponder whether KMT rule and black gold were really synonymous. The KMT had been fairly clean under President Chiang Ching-kuo's leadership and conditions were fast improving during his presidency. The KMT became mired in corruption under Lee Teng-hui. This came from an infusion of local Taiwanese into the party, most of

---

[40] Catherine Hsieh, "Corruption index spurs anti-graft fight," *Taipei Journal*, July 13, 2001, p. 1.
[41] For further analysis on this point, see Oscar Chung, "One year on," *Taipei Review*, August 2001, p. 5.
[42] Lin Yu-hsiang, "Prosecutors losing to 'black gold,'" *Taipei Times*, May 3, 2000 (online at www.taipeitimes.com) and "Corruption still a serious problem," *China Post*, May 22, 2001, p. 1.

whom had begun their careers in local politics where corruption was rampant.[43] It was also the product of Taiwan's prosperity.

There were other reasons for the Chen Administration not to press the campaign against black gold aggressively. One reason was that it was a very difficult task. Taiwan's legal system did not allow sting operations and the use of other mechanisms to deal with corruption. Another was the fact that many judges had been appointed by the KMT and/or were party members. They did not want anti-corruption measures to be aimed at the opposition. And they had the ability, as in most judicial systems, to slow down legal actions. President Chen tried to get around this situation by appointing a task force that operated from the office of the president. When he did that he was accused of an unconstitutional act.[44]

Meanwhile the press was not especially sympathetic. The media often called criminals holding office "spiritual advisors." Some they made heroes of sorts. Then the KMT controlled or influenced several newspapers, which regularly complained that Chen's anti-corruption efforts were aimed at other parties than his own and were thus hypocritical.[45]

And Chen had his own problems. Early in his tenure as president he appointed Peter Huang, a popular Taiwanese political activist, to a high level human rights advisory council. Huang was known abroad as the individual who tried to assassinate Chiang Ching-kuo when Chiang visited the United States in 1970. He was subsequently convicted by the state of New York of attempted murder. Adding to

---

[43] The NP attacked Lee on this issue from 1993 on. Also see Yun-han Chu, "The Challenge of Democratic Consolidation," in Steve Tsang and Hung-mao Tien (eds.), *Democratization in Taiwan: Implications for China* (Hong Kong: Hong Kong University Press, 1999), p. 152.

[44] See Copper, "Taiwan in Gridlock," in Copper (ed.), *Taiwan in Troubled Times*, p. 33.

[45] The opposition argued that this power belonged to the judiciary and to the Control Yuan. Most believed that they were legally correct.

Chen's image problem, a few months into his administration he was accused of a sexual liaison with one of his young, female advisors. The story became known as the "Lewinsky Affair" and had a much longer than expected shelf-life because Chen's vice president, Annette Lu, was allegedly the source of information about the case that was published widely in local magazines. She denied the report and sued one of the magazines guaranteeing more publicity and giving the scandal a longer shelf-life. Adding to these problems President Chen's son was reportedly given a legal position in the military even though his test scores were not high enough for the job and the president's daughter's fiancé was seen using a government vehicle even though he was not employed by the government.[46]

The other important "matter" that influenced Taiwan politically during 2001 and which became an important campaign issue was the economy. Chen Shui-bian had not campaigned on a platform of promoting economic development. This was the KMT's forte. By 2000, it was also taken for granted by the electorate and was an issue that was overshadowed to some degree by concern about the environment, welfare, and other "contradictory" issues. Chen stated during the campaign that he could manage the economy and that while the crackdown on black gold might hurt economic growth in the short term it would help over the long haul. He did not say too much about expanding the economy.

Taiwan economically, in fact, did well during the first six months of the Chen presidency. Economic growth was 6.57 percent (compared to growth of 5.4 percent the previous year). Unemployment remained low. The consumer price index rose only 0.33 percent in August. Exports were up 24.3 percent from the previous year. Foreign

---

[46] See "Chen accused of nepotism as son lands plum post," *Taipei News*, June 3, 2001, p. 3. For details on other issues plaguing the Chen government, see Copper, "Taiwan in Gridlock," in Copper (ed.), *Taiwan in Troubled Times*, p. 33.

exchange reserves were US$113 billion — huge by any reckoning. Thus the economy looked, and was, healthy.[47]

But this soon changed. The vicious fight with the opposition over Taiwan's fourth nuclear power plant was the catalyst. The opposition proceeded to impeach Chen. Although they failed, the fight worsened political gridlock and sent a negative message to the business community. The Chen Administration became seen as anti-business and did not, it seemed, have a good plan for dealing with Taiwan's energy needs.[48] By the end of the year the stock market had lost half of its value. Since stocks were used frequently to secure loans banks began to feel the pinch. Defaults increased exponentially. Private investment declined. Capital fled to China. The NT dollar fell and unemployment grew.

By the early months of 2001 pessimism about the economy abounded. Marking the first anniversary of the Chen presidency, growth of the economy was just over 1 percent and unemployment was 4 percent — figures not seen for 40 years. Labor protests ensued. Critics in Chen's own party decried the fact that Taiwan's industries were closing down in droves and going to China.[49] Business people were saying there was no choice. The government spent huge amounts of money intervening in the stock market, but to no avail. According to one poll, 60 percent of the population lacked confidence in the management of the economy. Lien Chan declared that the economy would have done better had Chen slept twenty-four hours a day.[50]

---

[47] Julian Baum, "Rattling the System," *Far Eastern Economic Review*, September 21, 2000, p. 78.

[48] Julian Baum, "Rude Awakening," *Far Eastern Economic Review*, October 2001, p. 16.

[49] See "Taiwan's industries going to China," *Taipei Times*, May 29, 2001 (online at www.taipeitimes.com).

[50] See "Chen's domestic record lackluster," *South China Morning Post*, May 18, 2001 (online at www.scmp.com).

The president's team blamed the KMT for selling stocks to depress the market and a stagnant U.S. and global economy. The KMT denied the allegations. The opposition then noted that Taiwan was doing much worse than its competitors and put the blame on Chen's lack of understanding of the economy and his poor leadership. During the summer and fall as the campaign gained momentum, the economic news continued to be bad. Exports took a dive. Growth turned into the negative column. Unemployment skyrocketed. Businesses complained that banks were unwilling to lend. Unions lamented job losses. Meanwhile the government did little to help. It perceived that it could not increase taxes to pay for larger welfare benefits. The opposition painted a grim picture and accused the Chen Administration of hiding some of the figures.[51]

In August, President Chen, almost in desperation it appeared, formed the Economic Development Advisory Council to make recommendations on fixing the economy. He called on business leaders, scholars and leaders of the opposition parties to give him advice. The latter refused to join, saying that Chen sought to cast the blame on someone.[52] They also realized that an election was coming. The Council called for expanded commercial relations with China. This looked to be problematic in view of the fact that President Chen was disliked by China. And it did little to solve the unemployment problem.

DPP political strategists continued to blame the opposition for creating gridlock and cited the U.S. economy and the global economic slowdown. After September 11, they blamed the impact of terrorism.

---

[51] "Slumping trade figures continue to plague Taiwan," *China Post*, September 8, 2001, p. 1.

[52] The KMT sought to start its own organization at this time. See Stephanie Low, "Lien pushes for meeting on economy," *Taipei Times*, August 22, 2001 (online at taipeitimes.com).

Shortly after, Taiwan experienced a devastating typhoon which made for more economic grief but also a new culprit to blame.[53]

All in all the political situation in Taiwan prior to the campaign leading up to the December 1 election looked to favor the opposition. Translating that into an election victory was another matter. Much also depended upon the campaign and how it was conducted.

Political Party Line-up and Platforms

Prior to the March 2000 presidential election, Taiwan appeared to be evolving from a one-party system to a two-party structure (although the country's party system remained technically a multi-party one).[54] A two-party system had been evolving for more than a decade. The Democratic Progressive Party had become regarded as the only party seriously challenging the KMT or *the* opposition.[55] Furthermore, a two-party system, many concluded, was a *sine qua non* for democratization to proceed to a higher level and was in accord with Taiwan's evolving presidential system. Furthermore, the KMT had come to recognize the legitimacy of the DPP and its role in the democratization process. At critical times the DPP and the Nationalist Party cooperated, for example in changing the election law to discriminate against smaller parties, and worked together to pass major legislation and even amend the Constitution.[56]

---

[53] See Myra Lu, "Typhoon cuts path of destruction," *Taipei Journal*, August 3, 2001, p. 1. This was one of the most destructive typhoons Taiwan had ever experienced due to the extremely heavy rainfall.

[54] It is very easy to form a political party in Taiwan and also to keep one in existence. There are no requirements to have a certain number of members or win votes in elections. The fee to register a party is quite small.

[55] See Shelley Rigger, *Politics in Taiwan: Voting for Democracy* (London: Routledge, 1999), pp. 28–29.

[56] See Jaushieh Joseph Wu, *Taiwan's Democratization: Forces Behind the New Momentum* (Hong Kong: Oxford University Press, 1995), chapter 5.

This arrangement was upset during the 2000 campaign when the country's most popular candidate for president, James Soong, was denied the nomination of his party, the KMT, and opted to run as an independent. Following the election Soong founded the People First Party and Taiwan's polity now had a three-party system, or at least one with three major parties. This structure was inherently, as it turned out at least, unstable, producing many of the difficulties and the political gridlock described above. It was especially troublesome when the two new opposition parties cooperated against the now ruling party, the DPP, which held only a third of the seats in the Legislative Yuan.[57]

In August 2001, another party formed, indirectly at least, under the leadership of former President Lee Teng-hui. This new party, the Taiwan Solidarity Union, was successful to the degree that it immediately constituted (tentatively for sure) a significant force in Taiwan politics. This was especially so in the context of the coming election.[58] The TSU was thus deserving, most pundits said, of the appellation "major party." This turned Taiwan's party system into a four-party one, or that is how it appeared going into the December election.

The party lineup before the campaign officially began could thus be described this way: the DPP on the left of the political spectrum, the KMT in the middle, and the PFP on the right. (The definition of left and right was based mainly on the issue of independence versus reunification with China though it also included views on taxes,

---

[57] Three-party systems, say many experts, are inherently unstable. In any event the KMT and the PFP began to cooperate almost right after Chen Shui-bian became president in May 2000 and made it difficult or impossible for President Chen to pass legislation.

[58] The TSU got one member. There were widespread rumors at this time that a number of KMT candidates would switch to the TSU and that KMT winners in the election would defect later.

welfare, defense, and other issues and was fairly consistent with the use of the terms left and right or liberal and conservative in the United States and other countries.)[59] However, even if accurate in describing Taiwan's political party lineup at that time such a view was confounded by the parties' switching stands on some important issues in the wake of the 2000 election and the DPP having to move to the center as a result of it now being the ruling party. When it joined the fray, the TSU was seen as a left of center party, left of the DPP since President Chen had moved to the center during his year-plus in office and the TSU took a noticeably harder line on independence than the DPP.

By the time the campaign got fully underway observers viewed there to be a "two camp" alignment, with the KMT, the PFP and the NP on one side against the DPP and the TSU on the other. The former was labeled the "blue team"; the latter was called the "green team." This categorization scheme made sense insofar as lines were fairly clearly drawn on the all-important issue of Taiwan's national identity. The KMT, the PFP and the NP espoused a "broader view" that saw Taiwan as part of China (Greater China or cultural China at least); the DPP and the TSU advocated a position called localization or Taiwan first. The two sets of parties or blocs were different in another crucial way: the former claimed to be and generally were, multi-ethnic parties; the latter were parties finding their support almost exclusively among Fukien Taiwanese.[60] In some respects Taiwan was back to a two-party (this time blocs) system.

Before the campaign officially started, all five of the parties just cited experienced serious problems that might have affected their

---

[59] Some would include the New Party, which would have been defined as hard right based on its stand supporting China's unification. Also, some disputed the view that the PFP was more conservative than the KMT.

[60] See Maureen Pao, "Independence Dream Team," *Far Eastern Economic Review*, July 5, 2001.

performance on December 1. In addition, intra-party and inter-party difficulties were quite apparent during the campaign. Both were more vexing than usual and an assessment of them and the various parties' responses, as well as the fact that some problems did not turn out to be serious, help understand the way the campaign unfolded and the election results.

The KMT, while declining in voter support for some years and losing the presidential election contest in March 2000, embarrassingly so, was still the largest party in the Legislative Yuan. In fact, it held a slim majority of the seats in the lawmaking body of government. The former ruling party, however, faced very serious internal problems and a shocking (to its leadership at least) decline in membership. Reflecting this situation the KMT lost a number of seats in the legislature between the last election and this one due to the defections of members to other political parties.[61] Finally, its public image was in tatters.

One of the most salient issues for the KMT was the matter of former president Lee Teng-hui. Immediately after its defeat in the presidential election, as noted above, angry party members demonstrated in front of party headquarters and demanded Lee to resign from the chairmanship of the party. Many blamed him personally for the defeat. The feeling expressed by a good portion of the party's stalwarts was that Lee had helped Chen Shui-bian win the election either because he wanted him to win or he thought that Lien had no chance to prevail and did not want Soong to be president.[62]

Lien Chan assumed the position of party chairman temporarily after Lee stepped down, but because Lien lost the election his credentials to lead the party were in doubt. So was his credibility to

---

[61] The KMT's representation in the legislature dropped from 123 to 110 from the 1998 election to just before the 2001 election.

[62] Many KMT officials that this writer spoke with at that time said this. It was the subject of speculation in the newspapers. Lee, however, denied it.

run for office again. Some party officials suggested that the party find a new leader, but there appeared no obvious choices. There were serious discussions about who the party should nominate as its candidate for the 2004 presidential election, but there emerged no popular choice. Lien thus remained both by default.[63]

The KMT's leadership, like most of the rank and file, continued to harbor bitterness over the election defeat. The party thus stubbornly refused to cooperate with the Chen Administration. Accordingly, the KMT was not disposed to be an opposition party, or at least not a loyal opposition. This situation, on the other hand, may also be attributed in considerable measure to President Chen's unwillingness to accept coalition government. Even though he appointed more KMT members to his first cabinet than members of his own party, he did not try to build a party coalition or reach any deals with the KMT on the distribution or use of executive power.[64] A standoff between the two parties resulted.

This "warring states" situation, escalated quickly when President Chen announced the cancellation of Taiwan's fourth nuclear power plant. The power plant issue and the attempt to impeach Chen which it evoked caused the president's popularity to plummet. However, the KMT's image was hurt in the process; in fact, its public approval ratings dropped more than Chen's. Citizens who viewed the KMT's performance as positive fell from the high sixties in the spring to the thirties in the fall.[65]

Meanwhile the KMT launched a re-registration drive from September 1 to the end of 2000 to "reconstitute" the party of only

---

[63] Lin Chieh-yu, "Lien gears up the polls," *Taipei Times*, March 24, 2000 (online at www.taipeitimes.com).

[64] Chen would have been marginalized had he agreed to the opposition's demands and, in his eyes at least, the 2000 presidential election would have been negated.

[65] See "Public approval of president sinks," *Taipei Times*, November 2000 (online at taipeitimes.com) and Dennis Engbarth, "The KMT faces hard fight for approval," *South China Morning Post*, May 21, 2001 (online at www.scmp.com).

loyal and serious members. At the end of the period the party leadership counted 850,000 members — dropping from between two and two and one-half million. The effort did bring back into the party heavyweights who had defected during the 1996 presidential campaign, including Lin Yang-kang and Chen Li-an, who had run against Lee in that election. Offsetting this, however, several other high ranking members of the party toyed with the idea of leaving. Noticeably those who returned were mostly Mainlanders or those who supported a one-China policy or better relations with China. Those threatening to leave were Taiwanese. The latter charged that Lien had betrayed Lee and had abandoned Lee's "localization" policy (meaning pushing a Taiwan identity as opposed to a China identity) of the party. The situation was so serious that there was speculation that the KMT would for sure lose its majority in the Legislative Yuan.[66]

Coinciding with the loss of members, some party officials charged Lien with a lack of vision and poor leadership. Outside observers said the party had not accepted the election defeat of March 2000, that no real reforms had been implemented, that the young were not interested in the KMT, that the party had no constructive plans, etc. Lien retorted that many of those who reregistered were young people and assailed former president Lee for having created the problem of black gold. Lien also boasted of democratizing the party rules so that the chair would be picked by the membership at large.[67]

In March 2001, in preparation for the KMT's electing (actually reelecting) its chairman, party operatives hired Jerry Fan, a public relations expert who was credited with having helped Chen Shui-

---

[66] "KMT exodus could cost the party its majority," *Taipei Times*, January 4, 2001 (online at taipeitimes.com).
[67] Lin Chieh-yu, "Lien gears up for polls," *Taipei Times*, March 24, 2001 (online at taipeitimes.com).

bian win the presidency, to develop two commercials for the KMT. The ads showed Lien Chan wearing a red headband and looking like an opposition activist. Many observers said they did not fit Lien's image. Clearly they were not successful in engendering public support for the party. The KMT's leadership, in fact, seemed to be desperate and grasping for straws while the silly (as some called it) public relations affair reflected malaise and disunity in the KMT.[68]

Shortly after this Lien was elected chair of the party in an election that was more democratic than had been the case in the past, yet according to critics was rigged or at least the qualifications to run made so difficult that Lien was the only candidate. Lien was picked with only a 57.9 percent turnout but by 97 percent of the party members' votes cast. Lien called for reforming the party bureaucracy and making the party more democratic and transparent. Little, however, was said or done about the "Lee problem." Former president Lee played golf instead of attending the meeting and did not vote.[69] In short, Lien was in charge, but his party was hardly unified.

Later in the spring the KMT held primaries to select its candidates for the year-end election. Decisions were based on a formula of fifty percent weight given to party members' votes and fifty percent to public opinion polls. There were charges of vote buying, especially from farmers' and other interest group organizations. But these charges seemed no more serious or damaging than such accusations in the past. The KMT, on the other hand, faced very real difficulties in reaching agreements with the People First Party and the New Party in jointly supporting candidates and otherwise cooperating in trying to form an opposition alliance for the campaign. The problems

---

[68] Lin Chieh-yu, "Analysts skeptical of KMT facelift," *Taipei Times*, March 22, 2001 (online at taipeitimes.com).
[69] Lin Chieh-yu, "No surprise as Lien wins election," *Taipei Times*, March 25, 2001 (online at taipeitimes.com).

stemmed both from Taiwan's election system and latent frictions between the KMT and other opposition parties.[70]

Meanwhile, some in the party advocated cooperating with President Chen. This seriously undermined party unity and discipline. Some lamented the bad state of national affairs caused by political gridlock. But many Taiwanese KMT members had other reasons: they opposed the KMT's moving back (regressing some said) to a one-China policy under Lien's leadership. The KMT leadership did not change its policies, however, except to direct more criticism at the president for doing little and talking a lot (calling Chen the "rhetorical president") and charging him with mismanaging relations with China and wrecking the economy.

Continuing turmoil within the party evoked rumors that former president Lee Teng-hui might try to form a party comprised of members loyal to him that he might entice away. At this time Lee regularly expressed his dismay at Taiwan's political paralysis, caused mostly, he said, by KMT-PFP-NP efforts to derail the Chen presidency. He said the KMT deliberately caused political gridlock and accused KMT leaders of reversing his localization policies. The "Lee matter" festered for several months and plagued the KMT leadership. Lien and others recognized that a significant number of KMT members agreed with Lee. Thus taking action against Lee, who also generally had a good reputation with the populace and a favorable public image, was seen as a drastic move and one that would hurt the KMT in December. Yet not acting was also hurting the party.

At this juncture, former president Lee published a book entitled *An Account of Lee Teng-hui in Power*. Lee stated in the book that Lien was responsible for the charges of misappropriating party funds made against James Soong during the campaign, which most observers

---

[70] Stephanie Low, "KMT flexes its muscles for election advert," *Taipei Times*, May 5, 2001 (online at taipeitimes.com).

said cost Soong the election. Lee also said that Lien had "broken his heart" when he asked him to step down from the chairmanship of the party following the KMT's election defeat.[71] The KMT's "Lee problem" got even worse as a result. Adding to the problem, Lee spoke disparagingly of Lien while openly praising and supporting President Chen Shui-bian and the DPP. Lee even said that the DPP, plus his supporters (many from the KMT) would give the pro-localization forces (later called the green team) a majority in the Legislative Yuan. This caused near panic in the KMT.[72]

In June, the KMT called for a "confederation" with China to resolve tensions in cross-strait relations that it attributed to Chen. This proposal was seen by some party leaders, including Lien Chan, as a means to deal with the problem of Taiwan's national identity and charges that the KMT had abandoned Lee's localization. The proposal bombed. It was portrayed (successfully) by KMT opponents as "selling out" to China. Beijing then nixed the idea, which it saw as a statement supporting an independent Taiwan (since a confederation means unifying two sovereign states).[73] The KMT henceforth stopped talking about it.

KMT's unity suffered a severe blow when it was finally forced to expel the former president and KMT chairman in September. Party leaders were torn by the decision. They saw inaction about Lee's bitter criticism of the party and his campaigning for TSU candidates as very damaging to the party. But they also viewed expelling the country's first directly elected president and KMT chairman for twelve years, and a person well known and respected in Taiwan, as

---

[71] Stephanie Low, "Lee's book stirring up discussion," *Taipei Times*, May 20, 2001 (online at taipeitimes.com).

[72] See Crystal Hsu, "KMT in disarray with treatment of former president," *Taiwan Times*, June 21, 2000 (online at www.taipeitimes. com).

[73] "KMT platform calls for confederation across the strait," *Taipei Times*, June 29, 2001 (online at taipeitimes.com).

an event that would hurt the party badly. The KMT was between a rock and a hard place. The issue divided the party and evoked reports that Lee would take members with him to the TSU and that the episode would undermine the KMT's campaign efforts in December.[74]

Going into the formal campaign period the KMT's election strategy was not clear. Its platform was not very coherent; nor was it agreed upon by its candidates. KMT compaign planners emphasized the negatives of DPP rule, especially the economy, crime and social instability, and Chen's poor leadership. KMT strategists reckoned that political chaos and uncertainty would be to its benefit as it had in the past. Party leaders, however, did not often offer positive goals except to say that the KMT was the "experienced party" and could provide leadership for the country at a critical time. Party spokespersons did not effectively parry the DPP's contention that the KMT had not adjusted to new political realities and it was the cause of political gridlock, not the DPP. KMT leaders made defending the Constitution one of the planks in their platform, but this did not resonate well with voters. Few potential voters understood these matters clearly. KMT objectives were not set out in terms of a very clear plan; rather they were mainly criticism aimed at the DPP and President Chen. Plans to fix the economy were the exception but they got lost in the midst of loud campaign rhetoric.[75]

If the KMT suffered from internal dissention and various other troubles, so did the Democratic Progressive Party. The DPP's travails originated mainly from the fact that in 2000 it and Chen Shui-bian had little experience that would help them lead the country at the

---

[74] See "Ex-president's KMT membership revoked by disciplinary committee," *China Post*, September 22, 2001, p. 1. Some members celebrated Lee's expulsion with firecrackers. Others spoke pessimistically about the event and some spoke of leaving the KMT. This was the first time a chairman of the party was expelled.

[75] See Stephanie Low, "Dec. 1 Elections: KMT goes on the economic offensive against DPP," *Taipei Times*, November 5, 2001 (online at taipeitimes.com).

executive level. The DPP was also a minority party in the legislature. Seeing the difficulties of belonging to the DPP, which held only a third of the seats in the Legislative Yuan, President Chen quit all of his party positions and vowed to be a non-party or "people's" president; still the DPP claimed him as its leader and his mistakes and setbacks affected the DPP. In a sense, the DPP had the worst of both worlds.

The DPP leadership also suffered various internal growing pains from the very start of the Chen presidency. Many DPP members were upset with Chen's policies toward China enunciated during the campaign. Some charged that Chen had abandoned the party's long-held and revered positions regarding Taiwan's separation from China or independence. They were troubled by many other things Chen said and did. Disenchantment also resulted from the effusive idealism espoused by many party members during the 2000 campaign and after that was dashed by the need to compromise once in office. Many had trouble giving up the traditional opposition and dissident role of the party. They were also gravely frustrated at both Chen's and the party's inability to get anything done with virtually none of the party's agenda being put into law.[76]

Chen also experienced difficulties with his vice-president. Annette Lu sought to be an involved vice president and her actions and policies often collided with those of the president and his close advisors. Lu frequently expressed publicly her unhappiness with the way she was treated. In the spring she wrote about her disappointments in a book that upset President Chen and many DPP members.[77] President Chen was severely frustrated by the KMT-PFP alignment

---

[76] Taiwan's newspapers carried articles on the first anniversary of the Chen Administration in May. Many of them wrote about this theme.

[77] Lin Mei-chun, "Critics say Lu's book untimely," *Taipei Times*, May 14, 2001 (online at Taipeitimes.com).

against his agenda and their frequent criticism of his lack of leadership. His presidency was likewise hurt badly by the economy deteriorating six months after he came into office.

But Chen was usually able to put a good face on his Administration's efforts to try to do a good job, making most people believe that he should be given a chance to govern. The DPP adjusted to its ruling party role and fared better in the public eye as the months passed. It also learned from its mistakes and profited from KMT disarray and campaign errors. Finally, it took advantage of President Chen's ability to communicate with the public.

In mid-2001, when reports circulated to the effect that former president Lee Teng-hui might start a new political party, DPP leaders expressed concern. DPP officials thought that Lee's party would compete with, and possibly hurt, the DPP in the voting in December. There was also some opposition in the party to cooperating with Lee (seen as the former head of the KMT and the creator of black gold). As time passed, however, most party leaders came to see bigger advantages than disadvantages in Lee forming a new party. Certainly President Chen espoused this view.[78]

In mid-July, top party leaders met to plan an election strategy. They decided on large rallies in August and September, the formulation of new issues, and a media blitz. One of the party's new issues, or, more accurately, President Chen's, was a campaign to improve efficiency in government. Chen called for cutting the size of government, putting an emphasis on reducing the number of members of the Legislative Yuan from 225 to 146 in the name of efficiency, and cost cutting. Chen coincidently appeared to be devising ways for dealing with the declining economy, which seemed to be a DPP vulnerability. DPP spokespersons, meanwhile, spent considerable

---

[78] Lin Chieh-yu, "Parties scramble as Lee's new party prepares to take their voters," *Taipei Times*, July 9, 2001 (online at taipeitimes.com).

effort putting out the message that the economic downturn was the product of KMT machinations, political gridlock caused by the opposition parties, and a downturn in the U.S. and global economies, rather than DPP bad governance. Following up on this issue, President Chen proposed an economic advisory group be formed to discuss the economy. He invited leaders of the opposition parties, scholars, and experts from outside and others to participate. In the meantime DPP officials appeared to calculate that President Chen was not going to be able to boast of any improvement in cross-strait relations and the party should perhaps instead try to exploit bad relations and maybe even provoke tension with Beijing. Party leaders at this time thus began to talk about China's efforts to hurt Taiwan's economy and to buy influence with the media, pointing directly to the effort to create negative news about Taiwan that would weaken the government.[79]

During the summer, party planners made a serious gaffe: They published a party advertisement that called for the youth of Taiwan to learn from historical persons who struggled to attain success, suggesting they learn from "model people." The four persons cited were Lee Teng-hui, John F. Kennedy, Fidel Castro and Adolf Hitler. The DPP later recanted the proposal, but not before the foreign community in Taiwan and Jewish organizations elsewhere condemned the DPP for its "bad judgement" or worse.[80] Aboriginal groups in Taiwan joined the fray, attacking the DPP for bias against them. The KMT and the PFP later labeled the DPP an "ethnic" party and one that was "playing the race card" in the election.

While the KMT and the DPP experienced serious problems immediately after the 2000 election that appeared likely to influence

---

[79] See "Media manipulation insidious," *Taipei Times*, July 11, 2001 (online at taipeitimes.com).

[80] Chuang Chi-ting, "DPP's Hitler ad creates stir," *Taipei Times*, July 12, 2002 (online at www.taipeitimes.com).

their performance in the December 2001 election, the People First Party seemed to avoid major problems. In the first nine months of the party's existence, it recruited ten thousand new members a month. Among them were nineteen members of the Legislative Yuan. In the meantime, its legislators were regarded the best in political performance and interpellation. Public support for the party at various times almost equaled that of the DPP.[81]

In January 2001, the PFP received good news when prosecutors announced that the charges brought against James Soong during the 2000 presidential campaign were being dropped. The evidence of Soong embezzling money from the KMT or acting in a way harmful to the party's interests could not be substantiated. Soong was also said to be not guilty of forgery as contended.[82]

It was not all good times, however, for the PFP. The party saw its popularity drop as it cooperated with the KMT to block President Chen's legislative initiatives and, in particular, as a result of the attempt to impeach Chen following his cancellation of the Fourth Nuclear Power Plant. The PFP was thus seen as the cause of gridlock.

The PFP faced difficulties in raising money and in building a party organization. It witnessed frequent charges, basically true, that the party was a one-man party or was James Soong's personal creation. The PFP was criticized for trying to make deals with both the KMT and the DPP while exploiting both parties' weaknesses. In this context it was also assailed for "stealing" New Party members and of hurting that party. Finally, it was branded with some success by the DPP as a pro-China party.

---

[81] See "Taiwan's Coming Economic Winter," *Taipei Times*, December 19, 2000 (online at www.taipeitimes.com).

[82] See "Prosecutors not to pursue Soong," *Taipei Times*, January 21, 2001 (online at www.taipeitimes.com)

Going into the campaign the New Party promoted the quality of its legislative representatives and its seriousness of purpose. Its leaders depicted the party as a party of thinkers and intellectuals and a party that could resolve cross-strait tensions and prevent a war with China. It clearly suffered from a lack of strong leadership and effective planning. It did not offer many ideas in terms of a platform and was painted as an extreme pro-China party by the DPP and President Chen.[83]

Independent candidates had less to work with due to the formation of two new parties that had lucid agendas and good leadership. Many independent candidates were upstaged by one of the four parties or the heavyweights helping them, or floundered for lack of a program and an inability to attract media attention.

From the day of its founding, the TSU supported President Chen. The party's stated primary objective during the campaign was to win seats and thereby help Chen and his party deal with the political paralysis allegedly wrought by the KMT and the PFP. The TSU benefited from Lee's support, but this was seen by some as a weakness as well as a strength. Lee had his antagonists and it was uncertain how long, at age 79, he would play a role in Taiwan's politics. Also, some thought the TSU would hurt the DPP in the election. TSU candidates sought to play down this speculation and to ensure that it would not compete with the DPP.[84] To do that it sought in ways to distinguish itself from the DPP. Some issues it supported, such as Lee Teng-hui's "two states theory" (announced in July 1999 that said that Taiwan and China were separate nations), gave it a separate identity since the DPP did not support this policy. The TSU, in addition. took a harder stance than the DPP on localization and relations with China.

---

[83] For information on the New Party's platform and election strategy see www.np.org.tw.
[84] Lin Mei-chun, "Dec. 1 Elections: TSU's 'top graduates' must make a name for themselves," *Taipei Times*, November 5, 2001 (online at www.taipeitimes.com).

The Campaign

"Election season" began on Sunday October 7, the first day for candidates to register. A few days later, 458 had signed up to contest one of the Legislative Yuan's 176 directly elected seats representing twenty-nine geographic constituencies and two Aborigine districts.[85] The parties had previously drawn up their own lists for the forty-nine proportional representation seats (forty-one at large seats and eight Overseas Chinese seats). A record ninety contestants registered for the twenty county magistrate and mayor positions.[86]

The KMT fielded more candidates than any of the other parties: ninety-seven for the district legislative seats. Nationalist Party leaders hoped to win more seats than any other party. They also boasted the party had more qualified candidates. Party strategists, in addition, sought to defeat KMT members that recently left the party to join other parties, as well as to retrieve some local posts lost to the DPP in the 1997 election.[87] (The KMT lost seven of the fifteen county magistrate positions it held at that time and the DPP doubled its take from six to twelve.)

The DPP nominated eighty-three candidates for the Legislative Yuan contest. DPP strategists sought to avoid their candidates competing with each other and did not want to spread party resources too thinly. The People First Party sponsored sixty-one candidates and the Taiwan Solidarity Union thirty-nine. The New Party nominated thirty-two, hoping to get 5 percent of the vote in order to qualify for proportional representation seats.

---

[85] "Candidates rush to register," *Taipei Times*, October 11, 2001 (online at www.taipeitimes.com). On Sunday only 32 and 6 respectively had registered. On October 10, approximately 200 and 50 put their names in the contest. The registration period lasted five days. Many candidates selected October 10, National Day, to register or picked an auspicious day.

[86] For details, see Myra Lu, "Parties have high hopes for year-end election," *Taipei Journal*, October 19, 2001, p. 1.

[87] Ibid.

For county magistrate and mayor positions, the KMT nominated twenty-three, one for each position. The DPP nominated twenty-two, the PFP six, the NP one, and the Green Party one. The TSU did not nominate any candidates for these positions.[88]

The list of candidates made news because some well known personalities either registered or were expected to and failed to enter the race.[89] James Soong, who had earlier declined to be a candidate for a proportional representation seat for his People First Party, appeared on the list.[90] Sissy Chen, who had at one time been a spokesperson for the DPP and who was well known for her antics in politics and more recently as a TV show host, registered as an independent for one of Taipei City's districts. There were a number of other well known people or celebrities in the race. Lo Fu-chu, the Legislative Yuan's notorious gangster, announced he would not run.[91]

Some of the parties had early on agreed to jointly sponsor candidates, but generally this did not work out very well. In Taipei County, Wang Chien-shien of the New Party won a pre-election poll among blue team candidates and KMT and PFP candidates withdrew according to a prior agreement. This was the most well known case of party cooperation working, though the KMT's Lin Jih-jia subsequently opted to run as an independent in the race, thereby succoring the DPP. In the Taichung mayoral race the PFP decided at the last minute not to support the KMT's Jason Hu and instead decided to support the incumbent. PFP leaders said at the time that

---

[88] Ibid.
[89] Catherine Hsieh, "Campaign dominated by familiar faces," *Taipei Journal,* November 16, 2001, p. 2.
[90] "PFP changes tune, adds Soong to its list of candidates," *Taipei Times,* October 10, 2001 (online at www.taipeitimes.com).
[91] Crystal Hsu, "Thug lawmaker to retire from politics, "*Taipei Times*, October 12, 2001 (online at www.taipeitimes.com).

they were disappointed in efforts to jointly sponsor candidates. In Kaohsiung County the two parties could not agree on poll results and thus cooperation to back a joint candidate faltered.[92] In some less important contests cooperation worked.

The ruling DPP launched its campaign with a rally in the southern city of Taichung. President Chen, Premier Chang, and party secretary general Frank Hsieh addressed the crowd. President Chen called for public support to downsize the government by one-third, cut the Legislative Yuan by half, and make the DPP the largest party in the legislature. He also cited his administration's future goals: maximize stability, conduct political reform, rejuvenate the economy, and consolidate the crackdown on black gold. Premier Chang attacked the opposition for blocking Chen's program and cutting funds for construction projects that created jobs.[93]

The KMT began the campaign by forming an "economic issues troupe." Party strategists sought to draw voters' attention to Taiwan's economic plight. They blamed President Chen for the recession and criticized the DPP for "ruining Taiwan." Party spokespersons also boasted that the KMT was the "experienced party" and that it had a fine record in building Taiwan's economic miracle and promoting stability and democracy. Party leaders denied the KMT was making trouble or creating political gridlock. Party strategists described the KMT as the "middle party" on cross-strait relations. The KMT's campaign advertising was extensive and focused mainly on competing with the ruling DPP while ignoring other parties.[94]

---

[92] Joyce Huang, "Joint Candidates pose problems for parties," *Taipei Times*, October 12, 2001 (online at www.taipeitimes.com).

[93] Joyce Huang, "DPP gets campaign going," *Taipei Times*, October 12, 2001 (online at www.taipeitimes.com).

[94] "Political parties highlight their differences," *Taipei Times*, October 20, 2001 (online at www.taipeitimes.com).

Soong's PFP pushed the theme of ethnic harmony and government efficiency while calling on voters to select the best party. New Party leaders asked voters to pick the best candidates.[95] Former president Lee Teng-hui helped the TSU launch its campaign, claiming that it would bring the TAIX (the Taiwan Stock Exchange) back to 8,000 and reduce unemployment to 3 percent. Lee charged that economic problems were caused by an unstable political situation.[96]

The KMT at this juncture was still reeling from internal unrest relating to the expulsion of former president Lee Teng-hui the previous month. Just as the campaign was getting underway, the party issued a letter to its members criticizing Lee for being ungrateful, noting that he had been "brought up" by former president Chiang Ching-kuo. The letter noted that Lee had once called the party the "mother of its members." Some party members meanwhile assailed Lee for betraying the KMT and engaging in "low politics" such as calling Lien Chan "pathetic" while making a mockery of his education. Mention was also made of the TSU being headed by Huang Chu-wen, whom Lee at one time had criticized publicly for poor performance. Many members, however, did not agree and supported Lee, or spoke admiringly of the former president. Some were reported to be ready to leave the KMT to join forces with Lee.[97]

Lee retaliated by attacking Lien for lacking appreciation for Lee's helping him run for president. He spoke of "rotten eggs" in the KMT and of those who "regard the Chinese Communist Party as their grandfathers and grandmothers." Lee at the same time praised President Chen for learning quickly on the job and called on voters to vote for TSU candidates.[98]

---

[95] Ibid.
[96] Lin Chieh-yu, "Lee Teng-hui says he knows the way back to prosperity," *Taipei Times*, October 7, 2001 (online at www.taipeitimes.com).
[97] "Kuomintang letter slams former head as 'ingrate,'" *China Post*, October 8, 2001, p. 1.
[98] "Lee continues criticism of Kuomintang," *China Post*, October 10, 2001, p. 1.

The other political parties, notably the DPP, avoided serious divisive internal disputes. DPP leaders, instead, talked about the KMT's internal problems and spoke favorably about former president Lee. PFP spokespersons avoided talking of any intra party disagreements, played down failure to work with the KMT (especially in supporting joint candidates) and didn't talk of the dispute between Lee and the KMT.

President Chen used his National Address on October 10 to parry KMT criticism that he had worsened relations with China. Chen declared that his Economic Development Advisory Council had recommended lifting bars to trade with the mainland and that he was trying to improve relations but Beijing was not cooperative. He presented an optimistic view of cross-strait relations, citing Taiwan's pending membership in the World Trade Organization. Chen hinted that negotiations with leaders in Beijing would take place in that context. Chen also diverted attention from the bad economy by talking about vote buying and the issue of terrorism.[99]

As the campaign heated up, Nationalist Party Chairman Lien Chan attacked Taiwan independence supporters, saying that they did not love Taiwan and that if the DPP became the biggest party after the December election it would be "goodbye to Taiwan." At this time, Lien was said to be disappointed that the party had not successfully portrayed the DPP as a danger to stability. Observers, however, questioned if this "old campaign strategy" would work, especially if undertaken so late in the campaign. Lien also noted that under the KMT Taiwan's economic growth had been 8.1 percent annually on average and that under DPP rule it had been negative.[100]

---

[99] See Hsieh Kuo-lien, "ROC to strive for normal relations with PRC: Chen," *China Post*, October 11, 2001, p. 1.
[100] "Lien lashes out at Taiwan independence supporters," *China Post*, October 11, 2001, p. 4.

In ensuing days, all of Taiwan's major political parties experienced difficulties. The KMT, though, seemed to encounter the worst problems. Some of its members were campaigning with or for other parties, even its members of the legislature. The feud with Lee Teng-hui was hurting the party and could not be contained. The KMT had to purge some members and try to portray former president Lee as wrong about the party he led for twelve years.[101] This was not easy. The PFP faced charges of selling at-large seats and the TSU began to look extremist as former president Lee attacked the KMT using language not often heard in Taiwan political debate.[102] President Chen meanwhile seemed to hurt the DPP after apparently deliberately picking a fight with Beijing over Taiwan's representation at the APEC meeting in Shanghai.[103] However, as the "fracas" escalated in ensuing days hostilities toward China appeared to help the DPP and the TSU much the same way China's threats helped Lee Teng-hui and Chen Shui-bian in previous presidential elections.[104]

In mid-October Taiwan's notorious Legislator Lo Fu-chu (associated with the underworld) won the chairmanship of the finance committee. The DPP blamed the KMT for this happening. The KMT, associated with black gold as it was, became visibly upset and hurt by the event even though Lo was an independent.[105] KMT leaders tried to divert attention from the Lo case by leveling

---

[101] See "Kuomintang purges ranks of unauthorized campaigners," *China Post*, October 13, 2001, p. 1 and "Dissent between ex-president, KMT chairman snowballing," *China Post*, October 15, 2001, p. 1.

[102] "PFP denies 'selling' seat on at-large list," *China Post*, October 12, 2001, p. 1.

[103] "Beijing, Taipei yet to reach consensus on envoy to APEC," *China Post*, October 15, 2001, p. 1.

[104] "Taipei protests, calls Beijing rude, unreasonable at summit," *China Post*, October 19, 2001, p. 1. and "Taiwan boycotts APEC leaders' summit," *China Post*, October 20, 2001, p. 1.

[105] "Independent Legislator Lo grabs finance committee convener's seat," *China Post*, October 18, 2001, p. 1.

accusations at Premier Chang for "vote buying" when he announced an appropriation of NT$100 billion for Taipei County if DPP Magistrate Su Tseng-chang were reelected.[106] The opposition also seemed to be helped by trade statistics released at this time showing Taiwan's exports having dropped a record amount while the jobless rate hit another high.[107]

Late in October, two events transpired which appeared to help the green team. Prosecutors indicted a number of high officials in the Jin Wen case, involving a junior college that was upgraded to an industrial and commercial college, a deal which involved huge amounts of bribe money and other corruption. A former minister of education was indicted along with a number of other top KMT officials from the previous administration.[108]

At the same time the final work was done for Taiwan to become a member of the World Trade Organization. This injected further uncertainty into plans to fix Taiwan's failing economy. But Chen administration officials pointed out Taiwan had been preparing for years and was ready and that the event (with China also about to join) would provide the means whereby Taipei and Beijing would negotiate their differences and this would foster expanded commercial ties as well as more amicable relations.[109]

Less than a month before the election, President Chen provoked a controversy, some said deliberately, over Taiwan's relations with China. He declared publicly that he had never accepted the "92 consensus" (an understanding between Taipei and Beijing that there

---

[106] "Chang accused of vote-buying with grand election," *China Post*, October 23, 2001, p. 1.

[107] "Taiwan exports record biggest decline ever," *China Post*, October 23, 2001, p. 1 and "Jobless rate hits another record high," *China Post*, October 24, 2001, p. 1.

[108] "33 ex-senior officials indicted for alleged role in Jin Wen scam," *China Post*, October 31, 2001, p. 1.

[109] "WTO will not handle disputes between PRC and ROC: Beijing," *China Post*, November 1, 2001, p. 1.

was only one China while allowing each different interpretations). Lien Chan and other opposition leaders said that this had been clearly agreed upon and that it had laid a foundation for improving relations. Furthermore, Lien said that Chen had not long ago told the head of the Asia Foundation that he accepted it.[110] Shortly after this, the Mainland Affairs Council announced ending former president Lee's go slow, be patient policy toward China so that commercial relations could be accelerated.[111] Juxtaposing the two issues, President Chen sent a signal that he wanted expanded relations with China economically but not politically. This seemed to accord with public opinion and put the KMT on the defensive.[112]

At this time President Chen reiterated his call for cutting the size of government (in order to save money in the context of a flagging economy), promised coalition government after the election (which appeared to be a necessary concession to end gridlock), and hit the KMT for allegedly planning to cut welfare funds.[113] The KMT did not provide a good response to any of these proposals. In fact, the KMT's campaign did not appear to be well planned and did not seem to be operating very well, though some KMT strategists said their campaign was working well locally.[114]

---

[110] "I never said I accepted '92 consensus', says Chen," *China Post*, November 6, 2001, p. 1. While there seemed to have been an understanding and it paved the way for formal talks in Singapore the next year, there was never anything put in writing on the matter.

[111] "MAC announces end to 'go slow, be patient' policy," *China Post*, November 8, 2001, p. 1.

[112] One official told this writer that Chen was carefully paying attention to the public opinion polls when he made these policy statements.

[113] See "DPP weighs up options for coalition gov't," *China Post*, November 15, 2001, p. 1 and "KMT refutes claims of welfare budget cuts," *China Post*, November 15, 2001, p. 1.

[114] Some KMT strategists said that planning locally was the way to win the election. Their view seemed to prevail more as the campaign went along and as problems appeared in formulating good campaign ideas to use nationwide.

On November 20, the campaign saw its first case of serious violence when New Party candidate Ho Cheng-shen threw eggs at former president Lee Teng-hui at a rally in Yunlin County. Pro-TSU members in the crowd were angered and grabbed Ho and hit and kicked him. Ho suffered a concussion and was rushed to the hospital. A TSU candidate subsequently led a group of supporters to Elmer Feng's headquarters, aggressively protesting Feng's "pro-Beijing stand." Feng's supporters responded in kind and a fracas followed. Feng's daughter was run over by a car when she tried to stop the melee. She went to the hospital and later said that her injuries were deliberately inflicted by TSU people. TSU activists meanwhile burned a People's Republic of China flag before television cameras.[115] Though the media played up these incidents it is uncertain what effect they had on voters.

The campaign period officially started on November 21 and was scheduled to last for a period of ten days. The Election Commission arranged joint speeches of the candidates and other events. Activities related to electioneering were limited to the period from 7 a.m. to 10 p.m. The government provided free television advertising to political parties that nominated candidates for more than five constituencies or over five aboriginal candidates, and distributed bulletins on the candidates containing biographical information, candidates' pictures, party affiliation, and political views before election day. Public funding was also afforded to political parties who won more than 5 percent of the vote in the previous election.[116] Campaigning became more intense at this time, yet the fact that the campaign was entering a formal stage was not really very apparent to the man on the street since it had been going on unofficially for so long.

---

[115] "Dec. 1 campaigns get downright ugly," *China Post*, November 23, 2001, p. 4.

[116] For details on election regulations see *An Overview of the 2001 elections of the Legislators and County Magistrates and Provincial Municipality Mayors* (Taipei: Central Election Commission, 2001).

In the heat of the final days of the campaign some issues took on greater salience as party leaders enunciated stronger positions on a number of issues and resorted to personal attacks and partisan appeals. The KMT, for example, mocked Vice President Annette Lu for saying that Taiwan joining the World Trade Organization would lead to membership in the United Nations. Other officials and foreign scholars agreed that this idea was nonsense.[117] The KMT also called on former members to "come home." However, this hurt relations with other "blue team" parties and was seemingly ineffective in getting any members who had gone to the DPP or TSU to return.[118]

At this juncture a widely watched TV debate between the blue team's jointly sponsored candidate for Taipei County magistrate attracted much voter attention. The blue team's Wang Chien-shien (a former finance minister and New Party leader), a formidable campaigner and a good debater, attacked the DPP incumbent Su Tseng-chang for buying votes by paying county chiefs to work on the election and blasted his party for mismanaging the economy and doing little to repair recent typhoon damage. Su and DPP leaders in response accused Wang of having "mainland colors." They also tried to split the blue team by pushing Taiwan's identity to appeal to KMT Taiwanese.[119] Observers felt this campaign debate mirrored the feelings of the overall campaign.

A subsequent DPP broadside against the KMT used a CNN report by Willy Lo-lap Lam that charged KMT leaders had asked China to refrain from dealing with President Chen and the DPP at this time,

---

[117] "A vain attempt," *China Post*, November 19, 2001, p. 2.
[118] "KMT chairman says former members should 'come home,'" *China Post*, November 19, 2001, p. 1.
[119] "County poll litmus test for presidential race," *China Post*, November 19, 2001, p. 4.

concluding that the KMT and the Chinese Communist Party were conspiring to influence the election. KMT, PFP and NP officials denied that they were receiving any support from Beijing during the campaign and said that Lam's report was wrong. They further declared that the DPP was trying to exploit the situation by "churning the report." [120] Officials from the DPP denied this.[121]

The next day the KMT issued a report complaining that the DPP was selectively making charges of vote buying against KMT candidates even though the DPP was doing it noting that the first vote buying conviction was a DPP candidate. A KMT official called this campaign "green terror." [122] Indeed, the DPP found the buying of votes a good campaign issue.

The Chen Administration not only launched an anti-vote buying campaign but also tried to investigate the KMT's assets, charging that much of its money was obtained illegally when Taiwan came under Nationalist Chinese rule at the end of World War II. The DPP said that the KMT got much of its more than US$2 billion in party funds from Japanese assets that should have been government property. DPP spokespersons also asserted that the KMT subsequently took control of more than two hundred Taiwan firms, many of them it still owns or controls. DPP officials asked for an accounting of the money and that it be returned to the rightful owners.[123]

On the campaign trail, many candidates went to temples or organized parades in their districts. Campaign advertisements,

---

[120] "Opposition refute CNN claim mainland backing KMT, PFP," *China Post*, November 23, 2001, p. 4.
[121] "DPP denies churning recent Beijing opposition support rumor mill," *China Post*, November 23, 2001, p. 4.
[122] "Vote-buying charges are a cover-up by DPP, says KMT, " *China Post*, November 24, 2001, p. 4.
[123] "MOJ cleared to draft bill to deal with KMT assets," *China Post*, November 20, 2001, p. 4.

placards, and ornaments proliferated. KMT officials predicted that it would do better than the DPP by ten seats in the legislative election. The DPP forecast that it would get eighty-four seats or about the same number as the KMT.[124] Some independents tried to help each other, but they did not form any formal organizations as they had in past elections. Shih Ming-teh and Sissy Chen campaigned together in Taipei.

Lien Chan reiterated charges that the DPP was incapable of governing. He and party spokespersons even called on Premier Chang to step down in view of the country's terrible economy and record high unemployment.[125] Lien also charged President Chen's interpretation of the "92 consensus" contrary to Chen's interpretation meant accepting China's "one country, two systems" idea. He said Chen's position stemmed from his pro-independence thinking and was a distortion of what had been agreed upon.[126] The DPP responded by charging that the KMT had been the main culprit in causing the political gridlock that was destroying the country and the KMT was not concerned with the nation's interests. President Chen and others restated their calls for political reform and added that the party would push to lower the voting age in Taiwan to eighteen from the current twenty to appeal to young voters.[127]

President Chen, former president Lee Teng-hui, and Lien Chan all talked about forming organizations to recommend and implement political reform after the election. Some said they all assumed that

---

[124] "DPP predicts even share of seats with KMT," *China Post*, November 22, 2001, p. 4.

[125] Iya Chen, "DPP, KMT wage war of words over governing capability," *Taiwan News*, November 29, 2001, p. 2.

[126] Amber Wang, "KMT chair stresses '1992 consensus,'" *Taiwan News*, November 28, 2001, p. 3.

[127] "Chen implies Lien is obstacle to plans," and "DPP vows to push for lower voting age to 18," both in *Taiwan News*, November 29, 2001, p. 3.

the election would not be decisive and that some winners might switch parties after the election. Chen talked of a "cross party alliance for national stability." Lee formed an organization called Taiwan Advocates. Lien said he planned to establish a "league" to safeguard the ROC's Constitution.[128]

Probably the most important "event" of the campaign, looking at the results in retrospect, was the DPP's decision to advertise vote allocation procedures in Taiwan's largest newspapers just before the election. The announcements told voters which candidate to vote for using the last number of their household registry as indicating the candidate they should choose. While not illegal, many felt the action was unethical.[129] The KMT did not do this so openly or, as it turned out, so effectively.[130]

Less than a week before the voting, the KMT again called on Premier Chang Chun-hsiung to resign over the "terrible economic mess" in Taiwan. Lien Chan noted that Taiwan's economic growth rate, stock prices, export orders, and domestic investments were all down and blamed the Chen Administration for this.[131]

Toward the end of the campaign period the candidates and party leaders (including President Chen Shui-bian) engaged in name-calling, made hostile statements, and used negative advertising. President Chen, for example, suggested that Lien Chan was finished

---

[128] Ibid. Also see Jin Yang, "KMT to build coalition to counter Chen's alliance," *Taipei News*, November 30, 2001, p. 1.

[129] Some DPP officials and supporters I talked to at that time said that the Party had long condemned the voting system which made this necessary. It also constituted, they said, taking away the voters' choice in voting and was undemocratic. Most, however, saw it simply as part of the process.

[130] KMT officials that I spoke to said that this would not work for the KMT since their voters were more intelligent, less partisan, and would see such an action as authoritarian and cynical.

[131] Sofia Wu, "KMT calls for replacement of Premier Chang," *China Post*, November 26, 2001, p. 1.

as head of the KMT because of poor leadership and the fact that his party would probably lose a quarter of its seats. Lien asked Chen to apologize for shrinking people's property values by half, ruining the stock market, causing record unemployment, and disregarding public safety. The DPP repeatedly mentioned the KMT's ill-gotten wealth; the KMT accused the president of misusing public funds.[132] Former president Lee Teng-hui declared that Lien Chan is the "only person that compromises and colludes with China."[133] James Soong charged that some members of the KMT's "financial and economic staff" had "been in contact with President Chen" and that "green team" people in the KMT should be disclosed.[134]

In the final stretch of the campaign the DPP escalated its accusations of KMT vote buying. It offered as proof of KMT violations the fact that the Public Prosecutor Office had discovered that the KMT had purchased a large number of checks from the Bank of Taiwan and other banks. KMT officials responded that the money was used for campaign activities and that the DPP government was practicing double standards in trying to defame the KMT. They offered evidence that several corporate heads close to President Chen had taken out loans during the campaign and that this money was to be used for buying votes. They also asserted that money had been misappropriated from the National Stabilization Fund and other government agencies and called for an investigation.[135]

---

[132] Lin Chieh-yu, "President forecasts Lien's downfall as KMT leader," *Taipei Times*, November 29, 2001, p. 1 and "KMT chairman plans league to safeguard ROC's Constitution," *China Post*, November 30, 2001, p. 1.

[133] Haley Chang, "Lee says 'R.O.C.' title no longer exists," *Taiwan News*, November 30, 2001, p. 2.

[134] Amber Wang, "Soong warns KMT defections likely after election," *Taiwan News*, November 30, 2001, p. 3.

[135] Iya Chen, "KMT under investigation for suspected vote-buying," *Taiwan News*, November 30, 2001, p. 1.

The Election Results

The polls closed at 4 p.m. after which votes were transferred from the polling sites to the central vote counting headquarters. The final results were promised by 9 p.m. Trends could be seen by 6 p.m. and a fairly accurate assessment of the tally was projected soon after that.[136] Due to some challenges and close counts in some districts the final results were slightly different the next day.

In brief, the vote tally showed that the KMT had lost the election. So had the NP. The DPP and PFP won. The TSU, most said, did well.

It was clear from the onset of the vote counting that the KMT had not performed well. That night television commentators, political pundits and others called the KMT's performance "bad" or even a "disaster." The next day all of Taiwan's major newspapers agreed. One called the election results a DPP "slamdunk." Lien and other party leaders labellel the election results a big setback and promised a thorough assessment and party reform.[137]

In the Legislative Yuan part of the election the KMT won a total of sixty-eight seats (fifty-five district seats, thirteen at-large seats and two Overseas Chinese seats), dropping from 123 seats the party held after the last election (110 just before this election). In other words, the KMT had lost almost half of the seats it won in the election in 1998, more than a third in this election. Winning sixty-eight seats also compared unfavorably to eighty-five or more KMT leaders predicted they would win. In addition, the KMT received only 28.56 percent of the popular vote, compared to 46.43 percent in the previous election.[138] The KMT's bad performance meant that the

---

[136] The writer was present at the Central Election Headquarters at that time and observed the vote tallies coming in from the various prescints.

[137] Iya Chen, "DPP slamdunks KMT," *Taiwan News*, December 2, 2001, p. 1.

[138] Ibid.

KMT not only fell from the position of majority party but declined so much it would be Taiwan's second largest party behind the DPP. This election thus ended fifty-two years of KMT control of the Legislative Yuan.

Observers in the media and party leaders cited serious reasons for the setback. Some said the party had not reformed after its election loss in 2000 and that it had learned little or nothing from the previous defeat. Others said it had not organized an effective anti-green coalition to battle the DPP and the TSU. Former president Lee Teng-hui leaving the party was likewise said to be a serious problem. That left the party split and confused. Many said the party did not have a good election strategy and was outfoxed by the DPP using the "ethnic card" and exploiting local nationalist feelings to create the impression in voters' minds that the KMT was colluding with China. Some said the public believed what former president Lee Teng-hui said — that the KMT was an "alien party." Some said the KMT did a poor job in voter allocation, which was obviously true.[139] Pundits also said that there was a significant portion of the electorate that blamed the KMT for political gridlock in Taiwan for more than a year and the downturn in the economy. Some observers said many voters attributed negative campaigning and vote buying and other forms of corruption mainly to the KMT. One analyst attributed the KMT's defeat to the bad economy resulting in less campaign money to spend, which had always been an advantage to the party.[140] There were a host of other explanations, including Lien's poor leadership, the party fielding too many candidates, too much emphasis on local elections, etc.

---

[139] This was the first election ever in which the KMT's share of the popular vote exceeded its share of legislative seats.

[140] Shelley Rigger, "Taiwan Legislative Election: Green Camp Gains in December 1 Polls, Blue Team Changes Hue," Foreign Policy Research Institute, December 29, 2001 (online at www.fpri.org).

Putting a somewhat different slant on the KMT's defeat, some party stalwarts said the DPP defeated the KMT. In other words, the KMT did not itself lose the election. Its setback happened because of the DPP's advantage from being the ruling party: its "right" to use official news releases, government paid advertising, and other perks including its organizing selective anti-vote buying campaigns. The DPP indeed managed to put the KMT on the defensive and diverted voter attention from the Chen Administration's problems, such as the economy, to the KMT's obstructionism and vote buying. KMT strategists also asserted that the DPP had deliberately evoked a deterioration in cross strait relations in order to help their candidates at the polls, and "this worked beautifully," said one official.[141] Some spoke of President Chen's stellar campaigning and the fact the DPP's gaffes happened early enough in the campaign to be forgotten. Also mentioned was the KMT sponsoring too many candidates and the DPP having nominated just the right amount.

Still, the reality was that KMT performed very badly and it could not legitimately blame someone else or another party for that. Hence, as a result of what nearly all party members regarded as a rout, in the immediate wake of the election defeat there were heard sounds about Lien Chan's failed leadership and speculation that he would be replaced. There was serious talk, even expectations, of more defections from the KMT (mostly to the DPP), further depleting the party's strength in the legislature. Clearly the KMT had to seriously assess the loss and even its future.[142]

The only bright spot in the election for the KMT was its "minor victory" in the magistrate and mayoral contests. The party registered a gain in this part of the election contest, winning a total of nine

---

[141] See "Cross strait ties could be in crisis," *China Post*, December 6, 2001, p. 2.
[142] See Jin Yang, "Lien says KMT must reflect on losses," *Taiwan News*, December err 2, 2001, p. 1.

seats compared to eight which it held previous to the election. This number gave the KMT the same number of seats as the DPP, which dropped from a previous twelve positions. Thus one might say the KMT beat the DPP in the local contests. Additionally, KMT stalwart, Jason Hu, won the quite visible mayoral contest in Taichung, Taiwan's third largest city located in the central part of the island. The KMT attained other victories in this part of the election context but losses offset those wins.[143]

If the KMT suffered a shellacking, the DPP chalked up a big, even momentous, win. The ruling party won eighty-seven seats in the Legislative Yuan (sixty-nine from the district contests, fifteen at-large seats and three representing the Overseas Chinese). This was an increase of more than twenty seats. It transformed the DPP into the largest single party in the legislature. Coinciding with the seats it gained, the DPP won 33.38 percent of the popular vote compared to 29.56 in the previous legislative election while besting the KMT by almost 5 percent.[144] The only blemish in an otherwise stellar performance was the loss of three positions in the magistrate and mayoral races; but this was hardly enough to redefine the huge victory observers gave the DPP.

Most party members saw the victory as a big one and one having great significance. Party officials and supporters alike were elated. DPP headquarters became a ballroom for dancing and celebrating that evening after returns came in.[145] Observers called it a great day for the DPP and predicted Taiwan's politics would shift in the DPP's favor in coming months.

---

[143] "KMT takes nine seats in the magistrate, mayoral polls," *Taiwan News*, December 2, 2001, p. 2.
[144] Iya Chen, "DPP slamadunks KMT, "*Taiwan News*, December 2, 2001, p. 1.
[145] Chun-yu Lin, "Hsieh revels in party's gains in Legislature," *Taiwan News*, December 2, 2001, p. 1.

DPP leaders attributed the stunning win to the party's mainstream views, its determination to carry out reform, President Chen's outstanding leadership, the KMT's disarray and bad performance, and other factors. Some mentioned the party's astute vote allocation.[146] One winning candidate attributed the victory to the widespread perception that the KMT was responsible for the political gridlock that had plagued Taiwan for more than a year and the DPP's anti-black gold (including efforts at stopping vote buying) campaign.[147]

Neutral observers and opposition leaders alike noted that the DPP played the ethnic card very well. They also said President Chen "conveniently" caused relations with China to deteriorate — much to the advantage of the DPP. Further, they noted, the TSU had helped moderate the DPP's image in terms of the independence issue and relations with China by taking a much harder stance on both than the DPP.[148] This explains why the KMT, unlike during previous election campaigns, was not able to brand the DPP a party of independence, and thus dangerous, in order to scare voters. President Chen and the DPP also took a more moderate, centrist view on these and a number of other issues. Another big factor, perhaps the biggest of all, was the fact President Chen was a very effective campaigner for DPP candidates; being the country's most respected and visible person attracted press and voter attention. Chen also spent a lot of time and energy campaigning.[149]

Just as the DPP won a big victory, the PFP garnered as big a win, perhaps an even bigger one. The PFP more than doubled its seats in

---

[146] For the first time ever the DPP attained a larger percentage of seats than its percentage of the popular vote.

[147] Cris Cockel, "Party representatives interpret election results in Washington," *China Post,* December 5, 2001, p. 1.

[148] See Rigger, "Taiwan Legislative Election," supra.

[149] This can be discerned from the election rallies, particularly during the last days of the campaign.

the legislature, winning forty-six (thirty-five regular constituency seats, nine at-large and two Overseas Chinese seats). It came in third among the parties in percent of the popular vote won with 20.44 percent. Both in the percentage increase in its representation in the Legislative Yuan and total seat gains it did better than the DPP. In addition, the PFP won two magistrates' seats (having none going into the election), in Taitung and Lienchiang, and supported an independent in Miaoli that won.[150]

After the voting, PFP party chairman James Soong said that the most significant aspect of the election was that little more than a year after its formation the PFP had made a major mark on Taiwan politics. He attributed the victory to the party's work in bringing political stability to Taiwan, it being a loyal opposition, its good legislators, its neutral thinking, and its professionalism. Soong also spoke of resolving Taiwan's political malaise. Independent observers credited the PFP with recruiting good people, but they also said that Soong attracted a lot of public attention and support for PFP candidates. Some said the PFP performed a "miracle" in doing so well, being a new party, without money and organization.[151]

On the negative side of the ledger, the PFP did not obtain quite enough votes for Soong to get an at-large seat, though party members said this was not important.[152] And the PFP's jointly-supported (with the KMT and NP) candidate, Wang Chien-shien, in the Taipei magistrate race lost. Some other joint efforts with the KMT and NP were disappointing. Finally, some said the party would probably

---

[150] Amber Wang, "PFP wins magistrate seats in Taitung and Lienchiang," *Taiwan News*, December 2, 2001, p. 2.

[151] Amber Wang, "PFP pledges loyal service as opposition in Legislature," *Taiwan News*, December 2, 2001, p. 2.

[152] PFP officials said that a party nominated member or two would step down if Soong wanted a seat. Apparently Soong did not.

have done poorly without Soong's leadership and his efforts campaigning for PFP candidates. All of this, however, did not distract much from an otherwise outstanding performance by the PFP.

The TSU won thirteen seats (eight regular seats, two at-large and one Overseas Chinese seat). It got 5.78 percent of the popular vote, which entitles the party to government money. Because of its good performance the TSU is expected to play a significant role in post-election Taiwan politics. After the election, Party Chairman Huang Chu-wen said that he was pleased with the election results and that his objective of ending political gridlock in Taiwan would be pursued.[153] Considering the party was only five months old at the time of the election, this can be considered a truly unusual feat.

On the other hand, some observers said that the TSU's performance was not too good. The number of seats it won was less than expected given the fact that former President Lee was the spiritual leader of the party and he campaigned hard for its candidates. Its thirteen seats was also much below the predicted thirty-five to forty.[154]

The worst performance of all the parties was that of the New Party. Previously the third largest party in the legislature, the NP won only one legislative seat plus one magistrate position. It obtained less than 5 percent of the popular vote, which means that it will not be able to form a legislative caucus or qualify for government financing. Its hapless performance immediately evoked speculation that the NP would close its doors and would soon no longer be a part of Taiwan's political scene with its members going to some other party.[155]

---

[153] Haley Chang, "TSU chair declares results satisfactory," *Taiwan News*, December 2, 2001, p. 1.

[154] President Lee predicted this number going into the election and some observers said he was serious about this and it wasn't just a campaign boast.

[155] Lisa Wang, "NP meets with catastrophe in elections," *Taiwan News*, December 2, 2001, p. 1.

A host of reasons for the NP's setback were cited, including its support of China's one country, two systems formula for Taiwan's reunification and its fielding too many candidates. DPP officials were quick to say the NP was too pro-China and thus did not represent the people of Taiwan. Its failure was no doubt more complicated than this though.[156] NP convener Hsieh Chi-ta attributed the defeat to voters paying too much attention to party affiliation and not enough heed to the quality of candidates.[157]

Candidates running from other than the five parties just mentioned also did poorly. Three candidates from the Taiwan Independence Party all lost. Other small parties either didn't sponsor candidates or they lost. Only ten independents won seats in the legislature, a decline of eleven from the 1998 election. In addition, non-affiliated candidates won but two positions in the magistrate and mayoral races. Independents not doing well seems to relate to the larger number of big political parties active in the campaign and the fact they dominated the campaign, plus political stars campaigning for these parties' candidates and attracting so much media attention. Independents have typically been special personalities. They were in this election as well, but they did not get as much attention as usual.

Looking at the election in terms of the green and blue teams or blocs, the blue team won a majority of 54 percent of the popular vote. It also increased its percentage (compared to the 1998 Legislative Yuan election) from 53 to 54 percent. The green team, however,

---

[156] The author interviewed a member of the New Party who attributed its problems to the fact that it was too democratic in its organization and thus did not have leadership, that too many members were academics who did not agree with other members and thus caused internal bickering, its failure to design a good campaign strategy, and indecision about whether to try to put more candidates in the legislature or gain in popular vote (ending up doing neither).

[157] Lisa Wang, "NP meets with catastrophe in elections," *Taiwan News*, December 2, 2001, p. 1.

made the biggest gain: from 30 percent (that the DPP won in 1998) to 45 percent (the combination of the DPP and TSU vote). Small parties and independents suffered a big loss, dropping from 17 percent of the popular vote in 1998 to just over 9 percent.[158]

Several known or famous personalities, some of them independents, won. Sissy Chen, former DPP spokeswoman and a well-known television host, was elected. She ran as an independent. Interestingly, she participated in no campaign rallies and did not buy space for campaign billboards; instead she used television to promote her campaign. May Chin, also a TV celebrity and running as an independent, won a seat as an Aborigine representative. Chin played in the movie *The Wedding Banquet*, directed by Oscar-winning director Ang Lee. Popular singer Kao-Ching Shu-mei won as an independent. She stated during the campaign she was running to represent Taiwan's Aborigine population. Yen Ching-piao, who was convicted in August of attempted murder and corruption and who was in jail during the campaign, was also victorious. Yen had conducted his campaign from behind bars with the help of his son.[159]

Some celebrities also ran with the major parties. Former basketball star Cheng Chih-long, the latest of four sports figures to succeed in politics in Taiwan, was elected. Cheng ran on the PFP ticket. Though having no political experience, he accrued the third largest number of votes in Taipei county. TV anchorwoman and PFP member, Lee Yung-ping, was elected. Actress Wang Hsiao-chan, who got a lot of attention during the campaign due to her earlier reported affair with John Chang and who dogged him throughout the early part of the

---

[158] Wang Yeh-lih, "Elections the beginning of the battle, not end," *Taipei Times*, December 2, 2001, p. 24.
[159] Zep Hu, "New legislators, strangers to politics but not stardom," *China Post*, December 3, 2001, p. 20.

campaign, won in the same district Chang did. Wang was an independent.[160]

On the other hand, some well known and even famous candidates failed. They include "Formosa King Singer" Yeh Hsien-hsiu, two gay candidates who promoted homosexual rights during the campaign, Ko Szu-hai who ran his campaign pressing the issue of stray dogs, and Chen Yi-hsin, a national baseball star.[161]

Some known political figures won; some lost. Luo Wen-jia and Sun Ta-chien, current and past spokespersons for the PFP and President Chen, won. Both ran for the first time and got solid majorities. John Chang, illegitimate son of former president Chiang Ching-kuo and a one time foreign minister, won a legislative seat from the southern district of Taipei. As noted above, Jason Hu, former head of the Government Information Office and foreign minister, won the mayorship of Taichung.

Lai Shyh-pao, renowned for his work on economic and financial policies and representing the New Party, lost. Lai had not been known for espousing radical views on cross strait relations, which was said to be the main reason for NP candidates doing poorly. Elmer Feng, who had run for vice-president on the NP's ticket in 2000 and was known for his pro-China views, lost. Shih Ming-teh, former head of the DPP and a popular moderate politician, running as an independent lost. Convener of the New Party, Hsieh Chi-ta, lost. So did senior lawmakers from the KMT, Hong Yu-chin and Pan Wei-kang. Observers blamed vote allocation for the large number of well known and well regarded political leaders losing and lamented the fact that most of these candidates looked like easy winners, led in the polls, and should have won. Many criticized the system for

---

[160] Sandy Huang, "Celebrities are among election victors," *Taipei Times*, December 2, 2001, p. 20.
[161] Ibid.

this. Some proposed that the law prohibiting the publication of opinion polls in the last ten days of the campaign be changed to prevent this.[162] Some called for a new electoral system that would eliminate vote allocation.

The quality of the winning candidates in many respects was lower than perhaps any recent election. This was partly a result of the voting system that favors single issue candidates and the use of emotional appeals (seen in past elections but present more in this one), the breakdown of the patronage machine, less attention given to candidates' qualifications to run for office, the ethnic factor in voting, and a number of other factors.[163]

The voter turnout was also low: just over 66 percent. In fact, it was one of the lowest on record. Voter apathy was no doubt the product of cynicism produced by months of gridlock and political bickering before the election. It was also a result of the nasty campaign that irked some voters. In some areas the favorite candidate not getting the nomination of one of the major parties was a cause. This obviously happened in the voting for mayors in Taichung and Tainan.[164]

Incumbents did not do very well. Among the directly elected legislators serving at the time 142 ran for reelection; ninety-two won and fifty lost.[165] Candidates sponsored by more than one party did not fare well. Wang Chien-shien, representing the KMT, PFP and NP, ran for magistrate of Taipei County, the largest district in Taiwan, and lost to Su Tseng-chang, the DPP's candidate. Wang was the most visible of the jointly-sponsored candidates. Some jointly sponsored

---

[162] Hsieh Kuo-lien, "Several political stars fail in reelection bids," *China Post*, December 3, 2001, p. 20.
[163] See "A Muddled Result," *Asian Wall Street Journal*, December 3, 2001, p. 6.
[164] "Lessons of the election," *China Post*, December 2, 2001, p. 2.
[165] "A summary of 2001 Taiwan elections," *China Post*, December 3, 2001, p. 19. In the 1995 legislative election, only 22 incumbents were not reelected.

candidates won, but generally party cooperation in fielding candidates did not work well.[166]

In terms of geographical breakdown, the DPP and TSU (the green team) candidates did better in the south, the same division that characterized the 2000 presidential election. The KMT, PFP and the NP (the blue team) did better in the north and also in the offshore islands. Regional voting tendencies were a bit less pronounced in the legislative races in this election but more pronounced in local contests.[167] The DPP did less well in urban areas than usual and the KMT did better. (The KMT won all the municipality elections, except Tainan.) The DPP, however, did especially well in Taipei and Tainan counties and in Kaohsiung City. The DPP did less well in areas where unemployment was high and in port cities that were hit hard by the recession. The green team won more votes from Fukien Taiwanese (those whose ancestors hail from Fukien Province). The blue team did better among Mainland Chinese, Hakka Taiwanese and Aborigines. These voting tendencies were also evident in the 2000 election and previous elections.[168]

China's response to the election was quite muted. The state-run papers for the most part ignored the event. China's official news agency, Xinhua, did not report on the results of the election, which meant that most of China's newspapers did not carry anything. Those that did took information from the semi-official China News Service but did not elaborate on the election with commentary. China's largest newspaper, *People's Daily*, cited the election results but with no details or analysis.[169]

---

[166] The electoral system was also to blame for this.

[167] Chiu Yu-tsu, "DPP loses support on the ground," *Taipei Times*, December 2, 2001, p. 22.

[168] See Bruce Jacobs, "Election results indicate intelligent vote patterns," *Taipei Times*, December 2, 2001, p. 22.

[169] "China's media mostly silent on Taiwan's election," *Taipei Times*, December 3, 2001, p. 3.

Beijing's silence was interpreted as reflecting its preoccupation with leadership succession in China and its leaders not knowing how to respond to the election results, especially the DPP victory, or thinking that it was better not to say much as that would be counterproductive. Others said that China was simply slow in making policy. Many opined that Chinese leaders perceived that Taiwan had become vulnerable due to the intensification of economic ties with China in the context of China's booming economy and nothing needed to be done immediately.

The Chen Administration conveyed the impression that due to the green team's victory Beijing would have to come around and negotiate with Chen and the DPP.[170] A number of DPP legislators and supporters contended that China should learn from Taiwan's democracy. Others said that China's President Jiang Zemin would seek to make improvements in cross-strait relations before he steps down next year.[171]

The opposition and foreign scholars generally disagreed. To them Beijing's response confirmed the view that the election would not help improve cross strait ties and that Taipei-Beijing relations would probably remain strained. Some noted that the DPP did not have a majority in the legislature and surmised that Beijing would wait to see what happened after the election. Some said, contrary to the DPP's interpretation, that domestic politics in China contained some uncertainty caused by the issue of succession and in that context a Taiwan policy change would be unlikely. Others opined that China felt no reason to make any concessions and views time as being on

---

[170] See "Policy toward mainland China will not change, MAC says," *China Post*, December 3, 20001, p. 1.
[171] Tsai Ting-I, "Scholars say that Beijing must grasp Taiwan democracy," *Taipei Times*, December 3, 2001, p. 3.

its side regarding the Taiwan issue because of China's economic boom and Taiwan's increasing dependency on China's market.[172]

The U.S. response to the election was very positive. The Department of State issued a statement saying that the election was evidence of the strength of Taiwan's democracy and signaled better Washington-Taipei relations. State Department spokesperson Susan Pittman said: "This is a tribute to the people of Taiwan." State's response contrasts with that of the Clinton Administration when Chen Shui-bian won the presidency in March 2000. That response was delayed several hours and was qualified with concern (or perhaps better stated, apprehension) about cross-strait relations. However, the U.S. government, as to be expected, did not make any comment on the results of the voting or winners and losers.[173]

However, neither the U.S. nor the international media made much of the election. Attention was focused too much on the war on terrorism and events in Afghanistan. In addition, it seemed to be the view of the media that this election, being a legislative contest, was less important. Certainly it was less exciting to foreign reporters than the 2000 election.[174]

The *Wall Street Journal* reported the election as a historic loss for the Nationalist Party and a part of a continuing power shift.[175] *USA Today*, covering the event in only one paragraph, focused on the opposition's post-election rejection of Chen's proposal for an alliance.[176] The *New York Times* called the election results a rout for the KMT and attributed its loss to party corruption. It also expressed

---

[172] Monique Chu, "Scholars see continuation of cross-strait stalemate," *Taipei Times*, December 3, 2001, p. 4.

[173] Charles Snyder, "US says elections show strength of nation's democracy," *Taipei Times*, December 2, 2001, p. 23.

[174] This writer spent some time with reporters during both election campaigns.

[175] Jason Dean, "Taiwan's Nationalists Suffer Historic Loss," *Wall Street Journal*, December 3, 2001, p. A16.

[176] "Taiwan opposition rejects alliance," *USA Today*, December 3, 2001, p. 7A.

concern over cross-strait relations as a result of the DPP's win.[177] The *Washington Post* opined that the vote favored Taiwan independence and China's reaction would be one of resentment.[178] The *Financial Times* emphasized the advantage given to the ruling DPP by the election.[179] The *Japan Times* noted that the election ended Nationalist control over the legislature and assessed the new situation this would create.[180] The *Economist* reported on the election and also editorialized, and in both interpreted the election as a major defeat for the KMT.[181] The U.S. editions of *Time* and *Newsweek* did not report on the event, though the Asian edition of *Time* did.

Conclusions

The results of the election, as opposed to what the polls predicted and what was anticipated given events and the political situation in Taiwan leading up to December 1, were quite different. The vote tally and the winners and losers (meaning the degree of gains and losses) among the parties were quite unexpected.[182]

---

[177] Mark Landler, "Nationalist are Routed in Taiwan Legislative Election," *New York Times*, December 2, 2001, p. A8.

[178] Philip P. Pan, "Vote Favors Independent Taiwan," *Washington Post*, December 2, 2001, p. A30.

[179] Mure Dickie, "Taiwan election reshapes political landscape," *Financial Times*, December 2, 2001, p. 4.

[180] "Chen's party ends 50-year Nationalist legislature control," *Japan Times*, December 2, 2001, p. 1.

[181] "On the brink," and "Kuomintangled," *Economist*, December 8–14, 2001, p. 41 and p. 12.

[182] The most recent polls taken before the election agreed with most experts. They predicted that the DPP and KMT would win about the same number of seats in the Legislative Yuan. Even after the election, DPP winners said that they had anticipated beating the KMT by only five or so votes. See Chris Cockel, "Party Representatives interpret election results in Washington," *China Post*, December 5, 2001, p. 1.

The explanation for this lies in four areas. First, and probably most important, the DPP and the TSU played the ethnic card very successfully. Both parties were able to win votes by appealing to Fukien Taiwanese based on their ethnicity. Fukien Taiwanese (or those who migrated from Fukien Province in the past) comprise around three-fourths of the population; getting a sizeable portion of their votes constitutes winning any election in Taiwan. The other ethnic groups (Mainland Chinese, Hakka and Aborigines) that together comprise but 25 to 30 percent of the population, in this situation, do not matter.[183]

Of course, playing the "ethnic card" leads to a divisive campaign and there are risks in employing it. But it worked quite well in this election. It was an especially good tactic to use in the milieu of serious questions that the opposition broached about the ruling party's mandate for governance for the previous nineteen months. It likewise made the state of the economy and the quality of political leadership much less important to the voter (who in an emotionally charged atmosphere was casting votes for someone representing his or her ethnicity) than would have otherwise been the case.

A second major reason for the DPP winning was the party's very effective use of vote allocation. There are problems as well in employing this tactic. It is not illegal; in fact it is perfectly legal and various parties employed it to some degree in most past elections in Taiwan. Thus, many candidates called it simply good or smart planning. However, it was condemned as undemocratic and unethical by some leaders in all parties, by scholars, and by many in the media.

In this election it worked better than usual for the DPP because politics had become polarized during the Chen presidency and became worse during the campaign. The DPP was also energized and

---

[183] The percentage of Hakka in Taiwan's population is not certain. It is estimated to be from 10 to 15 percent of the population. The Mainland Chinese portion is 14 percent. The Aborigines are 2 percent.

determined to win. It was more effective than it might have been otherwise due to the ethnic appeal made by the DPP and the bitterness that characterized the campaign. Many DPP voters simply wanted the DPP to win and did not care how. The KMT used it also, but less effectively because more of its voters opposed it and because the KMT was a party in disarray. The NP did not employ vote allocation — much to its disadvantage. The DPP's vote allocation success offset to a considerable degree the KMT's talent and money. Meanwhile the DPP had in some measure caught up in these two realms.

Third, the DPP very astutely spun the issue of cross-strait relations and, with the help of President Chen, turned relations with China into a political advantage during the campaign. Beijing studiously avoided doing anything to make China an issue, unlike in previous elections (doing missile tests during the 1995 and 1996 election campaigns and publishing a "White Paper" on Taiwan policy that changed its conditions for employing military force against Taiwan and threatening the voters during the 2000 campaign). Chinese leaders realized that they had caused a backlash in the two previous elections to the advantage of those that advocated localization, and intimidating Taiwan during this campaign would probably produce the same result.

The DPP, however, created a kind of China threat by accusing the KMT and the NP of seeking China's help in the campaign. Their efforts were facilitated by an American scholar and a well-known news reporter. The DPP capitalized on their reports. President Chen added the final touches when he made a major issue of Beijing's rude treatment of Taiwan during the Asia Pacific Economic Conference meeting in Shanghai. This worked. The China bugaboo also fit very well with playing the ethnic card during the campaign.

These maneuvers effectively negated the economy as an issue. But, the DPP was also fortunate in that the stock market rebounded at a critical time during the late days of the campaign. Moreover, some experts at this time projected a turnaround in 2002, thereby injecting a sense of optimism into an otherwise dismal situation. This helped the DPP. President Chen and DPP campaign strategists were also very adept in blaming the KMT and the world economic situation for Taiwan's bad economy. The president and DPP leaders were likewise effective in separating relations with China from the economic recession issue even though they were obviously linked. Alternatively one could say that the KMT failed to make a good case for it being able to fix the economy or liking prosperity and amicable cross strait relations.

Another reason for the DPP's win: President Chen and the DPP, with help from the TSU, used the issues of black gold and vote buying against the KMT very opportunistically. Some observers said that the KMT had learned nothing from the 2000 election. KMT strategists early on thought that the DPP would not use black gold as a campaign issue; they kept thinking this. Others did not believe the government's efforts against vote buying would be very productive. But, not only was the DPP's anti-vote buying campaign effective, President Chen literally "ambushed" the KMT by making issue of KMT assets at a critical time. Meanwhile, President Chen managed to avoid being tainted by his association with former president Lee Teng-hui, under whose leadership of the KMT political corruption increased. Helping Chen on this matter, KMT election planners perceived that making an issue of Lee was risky and would hurt their campaign, so they did not say much about him or about happenings during his tenure in office.[184]

The way the KMT responded to vote buying charges was also counterproductive. Throughout much of the campaign the KMT followed the DPP's lead in going after vote-buying. It said it was

---

[184] One DPP official told this writer that the DPP would have responded with praise of Lee Teng-hui's accomplishments in office, especially in democratizing Taiwan, had the KMT attacked Lee more, and this would have worked to the advantage of the DPP.

wrong and condemned it, but it did not find many listeners or believers. In the context of it otherwise failing to demonstrate leadership or credibility, this hurt the KMT's image. At times the KMT charged that anti-vote buying efforts were being aimed selectively at the KMT (which was no doubt true), but that did not convince many voters of it being unfair.

The campaign was dominated by political heavyweights to a surprising degree in view of the fact that none of them was at this time running for any office. President Chen, former president Lee, KMT chairman Lien Chan and PFP head James Soong were all central figures in the campaign. They often eclipsed their party's candidates running for office when out campaigning. This benefited the DPP, the TSU and the PFP. They each had a charismatic person helping them. The KMT and NP did not and suffered for that. It was said throughout the campaign that the heavyweights got more media attention than the candidates and they would influence the voting. And they did.

It was thought before the voting that the TSU would take votes away from the DPP and hurt the ruling party to a lesser or greater degree. This was a reasonable expectation; but it did not really happen. President Lee made it a central tenet of the TSU's (and his campaign) that the opposition (meaning the KMT, PFP and NP) deliberately and with malice had caused gridlock for the past year or more deliberately to hurt the Chen presidency and the country. Also, he charged they were opposed to localization and thus disregarded the national interests of Taiwan. Many voters believed Lee. Furthermore, the TSU, by taking a harder stance on independence, prevented parties not friendly to the DPP from taking the more radical votes from the DPP while enabling the DPP to move to the center. This helped the DPP. Lee's feud with the KMT, which distracted its election planners, in addition, made it easy for the DPP to make needed adjustments during the campaign.

Meanwhile, even though the blue team parties seemed to be cooperating and were engaged in jointly sponsoring candidates, in the end it was very apparent that they were mostly competing with each other. The PFP's gains were at the expense of the other two "blue" parties. This was partly a failure to cooperate. But, the nature of Taiwan's politics and the electoral system, among other factors, help explain this.

The above analysis suggests that this election should be viewed as *sui generius*. All elections should be; but this one should be seen as especially so. This perhaps indicates that the election campaign, even its results, says little about future elections in terms of election strategies or even winners and losers. It also says that the election may mean less about Taiwan's politics for the next year or so than might otherwise be anticipated. There are two notable reasons for this: First, the green bloc employed tactics that probably will not work, at least as well, again. Second, the blue team will adjust and/or learn how to deal with it. Political parties generally learn from an election defeat (the KMT after the 2000 election being an exception).

There is likewise good reason to believe that President Chen and the DPP (and perhaps the TSU as well) perceive that they employed below-the-belt, immoral tactics during the campaign. They may even have seen their win as tainted. After the election President Chen made unusually friendly and in some ways conciliatory comments to the opposition. He certainly did not do much gloating over the victory.[185] He similarly did not continue to try to provoke China after the election, notwithstanding DPP and pro-DPP media comments

---

[185] President Chen stated after the election that he wanted to work with the other parties to promote national stability and economic prosperity. Premier Chang agreed to resign with the cabinet, which is customary but is not required in the Constitution. See Ko Shu-ling, "President calls for cooperation," *Taipei Times*, December 2, 2001, p. 20. See also Wang Jenn-hwan, "DPP needs to heal ethnic divisions," *Taipei Times*, December 8, 2001 (online at taiptitimes.com).

to the effect that China would have to see the light and deal with the Chen Administration. In fact, just the opposite: President Chen made friendly gestures to Beijing.[186]

In counting winners and losers and assessing the importance of this election, all of the political parties, President Chen, and others concerned have to ask whether or not there was a voters' preference change. The evidence suggests that there was not, or at least not a significant shift. The blue camp garnered its usual mid-50s percent of the popular vote; the green camp gained considerably but this can be attributed almost totally to the factors cited above, especially playing the ethnic card and vote allocation. This election was thus only marginally different in terms of voter preferences from Taiwan's last five legislative elections. The fact that the DPP was declared a big winner comes from the fact that it did much better in seats than before (and anticipated during this campaign) and the KMT, its major foe, did much worse in both vote percentage and seats. The KMT's loss, however, also accounted for the PFP win.[187] The same goes for the NP's disastrous defeat.

On the other hand, the election results, notably the KMT's fall from majority party status, will have an impact. It means that Taiwan's politics may be characterized by coalition building. There is nothing in the Constitution about this and it has not happened before except for brief stints of informal party cooperation to amend the Constitution and on a few other occasions. So it is uncharted waters. It is difficult to say where this might go — if anywhere. President Chen's proposed "alliance" and others' plans for constructing extra-party organizations, including think tanks, haven't had many positive results so far. But it is probably too early to tell about this though.

---

[186] Tsai Ting-I, "Officials forecast talks with PRC within six months," *Taipei Times*, December 4, 2001 (online at taipeitimes.com).

[187] See Wang Yeh-lih, "Elections the beginning of the battle, not end," *Taipei Times*, December 2, 2001, p. 24.

In this connection one need ask the question: What implications can be drawn from the election in terms of it resolving certain issues or in forecasting Taiwan's future politics? There are several realms where it was suppose to have an impact; in some it did, in others it did not.

The election will probably have a salutary effect on the problem of political gridlock in Taiwan. It was certainly predicted to. President Chen had said this. After the election the president was obviously in a much better position to deal with the opposition and thus to govern. His party is now the biggest in the legislature. This is important. Chen will be a stronger president. He personally looked good during the campaign and helped his party win. This is particularly important. It will give him clout in dealing with his own party. It may help alleviate the problem of factions in the DPP. It will improve his image.

Yet one can hardly expect gridlock to cease to be a problem. After all the blue team won majority. Furthermore, the two opposition parties said after the election that they see themselves as the opposition. They may be a more loyal opposition; but they are an opposition.[188] Notably President Chen talked a lot about building a coalition after the election. This has not happened; in fact, the word was hardly ever heard in the weeks following the voting. Chen was not able to make a deal with either the KMT or the PFP. They were not willing. In any case, were Chen to pursue this it would hurt his relationship with his own party and with the TSU. It seems reasonable to think that this situation will persist. That being so and the fact that the opposition has a majority in the legislature means that gridlock will not likely go away. Even if President Chen or the TSU manages to draw some members of the KMT into its fold there will likely not be a stable majority and doing this will no doubt create bitterness.

---

[188] See Stephanie Low, "Lien, Soong won't join Chen's union," *Taipei Times*, December 7, 2001 (online at taipeitimes.com).

Another salient political question talked about during the months leading up to the election and during the campaign was fixing Taiwan's political system, its voting system, and the makeup of the Legislative Yuan. Are changes likely? Chen and the DPP favor a presidential system. The DPP's election victory should help them push the system in this direction. It should also succor their efforts to change Taiwan's electoral system and renovate the legislature. Yet to repair the system in any serious way requires Constitutional amendments and this will probably prove very difficult. At this time it seems unlikely. Such actions require the parties to cooperate.[189] Regarding a presidential system there is no consensus. There was no consensus before the election and the election did not create one. To change the voting system, which certainly is not a good one, means getting the votes of those who were elected by it. To reduce the size of the legislature will have to be a job for a future term since those just elected can hardly be expected to resign.

The election changed Taiwan's political party system, though it would be a serious overstatement to say it fixed it. The country now has a four-party system with two blocs in a multi-party framework. Most pundits do not expect the two green or two blue parties to merge anytime soon and the system thus to evolve back to a two-party system. Also, political parties are still easy to form. Consequently, more parties may appear. This seems to fit a parliamentary system better than a presidential one. Thus more change is needed, yet it is certainly not going to come easily.

This election, say some scholars, further consolidated Taiwan's democracy. It may well have done that. But it also sullied it. Playing ethnic politics and using vote allocation to win, not to mention trying to provoke an external conflict (if President Chen did that), do not

---

[189] In this regard, see "Strong opposition voiced against constitutional change," *China Post*, December 28, 2001, p. 4.

make Taiwan's democracy look good. The case can be made that there was devolution of democracy, not a consolidation of it.[190]

The election had an immediate positive impact on both the economy and the problem of black gold. The stock market rose after the election. Yet the economy was likely going to turn around anyway. Certainly it is influenced by many other factors than the election, including the U.S. and global markets and many other things. It is hard to say that the election helped the economy by much. Vote buying did not work very well and many perpetrators were punished for it. Others dared not do it. But it remains to be seen if vote buying comes back or not, or is replaced by something worse.

The election certainly evoked predictions about the 2004 presidential election. President Chen's hand was strengthened. His party won the election. He looked good campaigning. His poll numbers went up. Criticism of him by the opposition did not stick. Voters did not think that he was incompetent and lacked leadership ability as the blue team said. He certainly looks likely to win another term. He appears easily to be the strongest candidate among the pack. However, James Soong's (Chen's most serious competitor) position was also strengthened. Many observers thought that being out of an official position would cause people to forget him and his support base to weaken. His party's big win suggests otherwise. The KMT's defeat perhaps means that Lien Chan will not be a candidate in 2004. Ma Ying-jeou's ability to attract big audiences during the campaign suggests he is a strong candidate. Ma also found appeal south of Taipei where, according to the conventional wisdom, he had no support.[191]

---

[190] For details see John F. Copper, "Taiwan: Democracy's Devolution," *Journal of Contemporary China* (coming issue).

[191] Lin Miao-jung, "Survey gives high marks to mayor," *Taipei Times*, December 10, 2001 (online at taipeitimes.com).

These, of course, are generalizations. Two years is a long time in politics. If Soong and Ma both run they will likely split the conservative vote and assure Chen another term. Chen doesn't have to worry about this as there is no other popular candidate in the green bloc. Lee Teng-hui will not be a candidate.

One final observation: President Chen will now be seen as the one to credit if things go well, and blame if they do not. The same goes for the DPP. Thus, the next two years will be critical for both and the new political situation will impact Taiwan's democracy, political party system, and much more.

ABOUT THE AUTHOR

John F. COPPER is the Stanley J. Buckman Distinguished Professor of International Studies at Rhodes College in Memphis, Tennessee. He is the author of more than twenty books on Taiwan, China, and Asian Affairs. His book *China's Global Role* (1980) won the Clarence Day Foundation Award for outstanding research and creativity activity. Professor Copper's most recent books include *Historical Dictionary of Taiwan* (second edition) published in 2000 and *Taiwan in Troubled Times: Essays on the Chen Shui-bian Presidency* (edited) published in 2002.

In 1997, Dr. Copper was the recipient of the International Communications Award.

Professor Copper was a Visiting Senior Research Fellow at the East Asian Institute, National University of Singapore during the summer of 2002 where he finished this work.